P9-DZO-199

October 14, 1999

To my dear Tamara,

As I'm certain there will be no overindulgence with Sir Cal, I thought this would be an enjoyable reading experience anyway! From one brat to another—

All the best,

Wendy

I Refuse
to Raise a
BRAT

ALSO BY MARILU HENNER

The 30-Day Total Health Makeover, ReganBooks
Marilu Henner's Total Health Makeover, ReganBooks
By All Means Keep on Moving, Pocket Books

I Refuse to Raise a

BRAT

Straightforward Advice on
Parenting in an Age of Overindulgence

Marilu Henner

and

Ruth Velikovsky Sharon, Ph.D.

ReganBooks
An Imprint of HarperCollinsPublishers

The information in this book has been carefully researched, and all efforts have been made to ensure accuracy. The authors and the publisher assume no responsibility for any injuries suffered or damages or losses incurred during or as a result of following this information. All information should be carefully studied and clearly understood before taking any action based on the information or advice in this book.

I REFUSE TO RAISE A BRAT. Copyright © 1999 by Perpetual Motion, Inc. and Ruth Velikovsky Sharon, Ph.D. All rights reserved. Printed in the United States of America. No part of this book may be used or reproduced in any manner whatsoever without written permission except in the case of brief quotations embodied in critical articles and reviews. For information address HarperCollins Publishers, Inc., 10 East 53rd Street, New York, NY 10022.

HarperCollins books may be purchased for educational, business, or sales promotional use. For information please write: Special Markets Department, HarperCollins Publishers, Inc., 10 East 53rd Street, New York, NY 10022.

FIRST EDITION

Designed by Laura Lindgren and Celia Fuller

Drawings by Ralph Schlegel

Library of Congress Cataloging-in-Publication Data

ISBN 0-06-039266-5

99 00 01 02 03 /❖ 10 9 8 7 6 5 4 3 2 1

To Nicky and Joey
—Marilu

To my grandchildren:
Elizabeth, Ashley, Cimarron, Colby, and Dylan
—Dr. Sharon

CONTENTS

ACKNOWLEDGMENTS

Without the support, talent, and hard work from the following people, this project would never have been possible.

To Judith Regan, who continues to be my friend and idol . . . her unbeatable team at ReganBooks and HarperCollins, Amye Dyer, Angelica Canales, Rick Pracher, Steven Sorrentino, Paul Olsewski (who stops at nothing to get the news out), Renée Iwaszkiewicz, Claudia Gabel, Cassie Jones, and especially Laura Yorke, who showed me what a truly great editor does to save the day. I hope this is the first of many.

To Mel Berger, Marc Schwartz, Sam Haskell, Rick Bradley, and Jerry Katzman of the William Morris Agency, Dick Guttman and Susan Madore of Guttman & Associates, and Richard Feldstein and Barbara Karrol at Provident Financial Management.

To Stephanie Pierson for her ability to make order out of chaos, and to her husband, Tom Connell, for his tireless support.

To Brent Strickland, who once again brought his magic fingers and great attitude. To Trent Othick for always coming through. To Bryony Atkinson for her organization, speed, and great outfits. To Suzanne Carney and Charlotte Huss for reminding us what it's like to have an infant. To my sister JoAnn Carney for her exquisite photos. To Elizabeth Carney for her full-service troubleshooting. To my sister-in-law Lynnette Lesko Henner, who sorted, filed, and tagged, and inspired. To Caroline Aaron for once again adding her special brand of humor and insight inspired by her children, Ben and Sydney. And to my brother Lorin Henner—I said so much about you in the last book, I've nothing left to say, except that you'll always be my favorite brat.

To Elena Lewis, for her can-do attitude and organizational skills.

To Donna Erickson, who follows the principles in this book without even realizing it.

To Lorne Lieberman and Erin Lieberman Othick, who gave me my first lessons in parenting.

To my talented husband, Rob, who shares with me the great joy and responsibility of raising our two sons.

And to Nicky and Joey, who are the best reasons for wanting to be a good parent.

—Marilu

■   ■   ■

Thanks to Heather Menozzi for her long hours at the computer and to her son, Corey, for his humor; to Elizabeth Hartnett for her loyalty; to Marilyn Frasier for her organizational skills; to Lorna Sharon for her very thoughtful suggestions and recommendations; to Rafael Sharon, whose deep understanding of children makes him a great father; to Naomi Mitchell for her helpful insights and contributions; to Carmel Warner for her brilliant understanding of how children learn; to Dr. Robert Ginsberg for his exemplary approach to children's education; to John O'Donnell, Peter Shukat, Denise Johnson for their help; to Richard Peterson for his help; to Ralph Schlegel, whose drawings capture the human condition; to Stephanie Pierson for her creative expertise and to her husband, Tom Connell, for his help; to Laura Yorke for her editorial skills, and to Judith Regan, whose brilliance, energy, and determination have made this book a reality.

—Dr. Sharon

Marilu Henner

Being a mom is my favorite, and by far the most important, thing I do in my life. When I look at the beautiful faces of my two little boys, Nicky, age five, and Joey, three and a half, I know I want to be the best mother I can be. But what does being the best mother mean? Does it mean that I'm supposed to do everything for my children, and then one day expect them to be able to do those things for themselves? Should I try to anticipate their needs before they even know and can identify those needs? Does it mean that I'm supposed to shield them from all of life's bumps and hard knocks? And how difficult will it be for them to cope when I'm not there to be their shield? As a parent, you want to do so much for your children, but how much is too much? At what point does giving and protecting too much become what we will refer to throughout this book as overgratification? My parents, who raised six of us, often let us stumble and fall and find our own way. They had to. There wasn't enough time in the day for them to hover over and do too much for six children. We sometimes learned the hard way, and had a few mishaps along the way, but eventually we all had to learn to fend for ourselves.

My children are relatively young right now. As a mom, I know I'm a work in progress. I don't claim to be an expert yet. I am, however, fortunate enough to have had the guidance of Dr. Ruth Velikovsky Sharon. She is a brilliant psychoanalyst who has helped me in my career for many years, and the mother of three successful adults who have families of their own. The most important lesson she has taught me about child rearing is that the majority of problems we experience throughout our lives can be traced to being overgratified, overprotected, and/or overindulged as children. Giving too much to our children is one of the surest ways to deprive them of the emotional and physical tools they will need to cope with the many challenges and changes of life. Every time I have followed her theories, I can see positive results. And every time I'm having trouble, or anyone around me is having trouble, it usually relates to overgratification in some way. Overfrustration (giving a child too little) is the opposite of overgratification, and can also create problems in one's life. The answer lies in finding a *balance* between frustration and gratification. Finding that balance is what this book is all about.

The world is a frustrating place where every day we must identify what we need and what we want in order to get it. And sometimes it takes a long time to get it, or we *never* get it. That's life. Some people are better equipped to deal with life's frustrations than others, and that's probably because their parents allowed them to work through their frustrations at an early age. But so many parents today do everything they can to avoid teaching their children these important life-coping skills.

From the day my first son, Nicky, was born, I tried to apply Dr. Sharon's advice. I learned to listen to the differences in Nicky's cries. Eventually, I could distinguish his "cry to be fed" from his "cry to be played with" from his "cry to be changed," and so on. If

I hadn't let him cry *first,* I never would have been able to recognize the differences in his cries. Nicky and I soon developed our own "language," and instead of my anticipating his every need (which is an unrealistic way to bring up a child, because the world doesn't work that way), he was able to cry and let me know what he wanted. I was then able to help him.

When Nicky was around fourteen months old, I was explaining to Dr. Sharon that I was having a really hard time putting him to bed. He slept through the night by that time, of course, but getting him to bed was difficult, because early on, despite Dr. Sharon's advice to put him down awake and let him fall asleep on his own, I would rock him to sleep while singing my favorite Beatles songs. It was a time I looked forward to every day, but now the ritual was getting old, and with Joey on the way (I was five months pregnant at the time), it was exhausting. I remember saying to her, "I know, I know, I shouldn't have let this go on so long. He's too old to be rocked to sleep. It's too much, and he now knows he's getting away with something, too. I can tell. There's this bratty quality about it now, and I refuse to raise a brat!"

So, what is a brat? Every kid is a little bratty sometimes, of course. But when we talk about a brat in this book, we're talking about that uncooperative, whining, annoying, demanding, selfish little (or big) person whom no one can control. We've seen them all too often in malls, restaurants, theaters, and playgrounds. Their parents are constantly pleading and bribing and enticing and bargaining. Brats can come in all shapes, sizes, and even ages, because little brats often become big brats. Some grown-ups never stop being brats; they only get better at hiding their brattiness. Throughout this book, we will extensively explore these questions: What makes a child become a brat in the first place? And what can parents do (and more important, *not* do) to keep their child from becoming a brat? What kind of mindset do we need, as parents, to raise our children?

When I became a mother, Dr. Sharon and I started writing this book together. As a new mother, so many questions came up every day of my first child's life. And then, once I had two children and realized that the playing field had changed, I thought, How do I balance the frustration and gratification between the two of them?

We all want to do a great job as parents, but striving to be *perfect* parents is a mistake. The world is not a perfect place, and insisting on perfection can be both paralyzing and crazy-making (for us and our children). It's inevitable that we're going to make mistakes along the way. It's just that it's better to *have* a general mind-set, a sort of blueprint, even if we end up straying from it every once in a while. If we are on the right path, the results will be much better than if we had no structure, no boundaries, and no guidelines. That's why Dr. Sharon and I have written this book: to take you through the different aspects of raising a child. It sounds very simple to say, "Okay, I'm just not going to overgratify my children." But when you've got a crying baby, what do you do? When you can't understand what your five-year-old is upset about, what do you do? Or if you've got a twelve-year-old and some bad habits have crept in, how do you *undo* those habits?

The chapters of this book include a number of elements. I introduce each topic, and Dr. Sharon's ideas, written in her own words, follow. In each of the chapters, there is a series of questions we've appropriately called "Brat-Busters." The questions reflect the issues of the chapter, made real by everyday parents and their concerns. Even if a question doesn't apply to your situation, you may recognize your life somewhere else in the question or answer. In addition to Dr. Sharon's answer, I usually add my insight as a mom, currently and joyously at the frontline of motherhood. There is a brief section in each chapter about the consequences of certain behaviors if children carry them into adulthood. It's aptly titled "When Little Brats Become Big Brats."

I hope you find our book inspiring and helpful in your desire to become a great (but not perfect!) parent.

Dr. Ruth V. Sharon

As a psychoanalyst in practice for the past twenty-five years, my perspective on child rearing has given me some fresh views and insights that I believe would be immensely helpful to today's parents. While much of my advice about raising children might seem to go against the common wisdom, I have seen it work time and again, producing successful and long-lasting results and winning over even the most skeptical parents.

All my theories are based on one simple (and surprising) observation: Some of the most difficult patients I've treated have not been those who were poorly treated or neglected as children, but those who were overindulged or who received endless gratification and attention. Patients who, as children, were treated as special and entitled, whose parents did everything to try to keep them happy all the time, had more emotional problems and unresolved issues than children who grew up dealing with adversity and frustration from a very young age. Sadly, these same patients had a harder time in therapy, too—they made less progress and took longer resolving problems. Perhaps most surprising, these over-tended and overgratified children were the most vocal about blam-

ing their parents for a miserable childhood once they themselves
became adults, in spite of (or because of) the superhuman efforts
their parents made to make their childhoods idyllic. It is most disturbing to observe the emotional damage parents innocently per-
petuate on their children, while meaning well. The extent of the
damage can be far-reaching. But with some simple understanding
of a child's natural development and the right tools, it's fairly simple to be a loving *and* effective parent.

Developmentally, every baby, from day one, needs to feel loved
and nurtured and profoundly cared for by responsible parents. But
parents need to know that once a newborn comes into the world
and starts breathing on his own, he also needs to begin developing
a healthy independence from his parents. Too much nurturing, too
much bonding, too much togetherness will suppress this natural
drive to independence.

The trick is to find a balance between being there for a child
and giving him a chance to discover the world (not always an easy
place) for himself. Growth from gratification and learning from
frustration are equally important, but except in theories and text-
books, there is no possibility of achieving a *perfect* balance. Again
at the risk of going against accepted theories, I would suggest that,
no matter what the child's temperament is like, it is better in the
long run to err on the side of denying him than in overindulging
him.

I know that this is a difficult concept for a loving parent to
accept, but I've found that overgratifying a child is often the easy
way out. And denying a child anything these days is frowned
upon. Popular psychology (and a misinterpretation of some excellent psychological theories about self-esteem) have led parents
today routinely to confuse love with overgratification and to believe
that any amount of frustration is too much. Of course, every child

is different. Each child's temperament needs to be considered in finding the right balance of frustration and gratification suited to him. Genetic makeup will also predetermine some of his characteristics that will affect this balance.

Any parenting book that addresses the merits of frustration and denial of immediate gratification runs the risk of seeming harsh and unloving. And at first, some of the advice and suggestions in this book may sound a little harsh or unsympathetic, but it is just this kind of loving and pragmatic advice that will ultimately provide the blueprint for bringing up well-functioning children who, as adults, continue to prosper.

Marilu Henner's dedication to physical and psychological health, her vitality, intelligence, humor, and vibrant personality are evident from her contribution as coauthor of this book, which she titled *I Refuse to Raise a Brat*.

CHAPTER 1

Twenty-Four-Hour Womb Service

May 12, 1994. I remember it well. I woke up in the middle of the night and thought, "Today's the day." Even though contractions hadn't started, I knew that was going to be the day I would give birth. I immediately started reorganizing the baby's room, which is what most new mothers do—the whole nesting thing. I became obsessed with wanting everything to be just right for the baby's arrival.

When I brought my son Nicky home, I couldn't believe that only twenty-four hours earlier, he had been growing inside me. And part of me still wanted to feel connected. In retrospect, I think that probably had more to do with my hormones and my needs than it had to do with what was best for him. And just like a new diet, a New

Year's resolution, or the first day of a new school year, I approached this experience wanting everything to be *perfect*.

I'd already found the best crib, picked out the ideal wallpaper, organized all the clothes and toys and bedding that I'd gotten at my baby shower. I was bursting with joy as I picked up every little sock and T-shirt, not really believing that a whole human being could actually fit into those teeny-tiny clothes. Nothing seemed entirely real. During my pregnancy, I felt Nicky growing and kicking, but at that point he seemed to be more part of me than his own person. I think that's why his room became so significant. I realized that this was going to be the place where he would begin his own independent life, wearing those impossibly tiny T-shirts! He was going to be living in this whole new world and I was going to be the one responsible for setting it up. And I wanted it to be just right.

So when I got Nicky home from the hospital, it wasn't enough that I wouldn't let anyone hold him without washing his hands first. I even got squeamish if anyone had too much perfume or garlic breath or the slightest body odor because I didn't want my perfect baby, in his perfect world, to have to smell anything unpleasant! I remember asking everyone to be quiet all the time, especially my husband. I thought his voice was too loud for "my" baby.

Luckily, after a few days, I snapped out of this nonsense. Besides, there were too many people around. Phones were ringing, music was blasting, doors were slamming, odors were permeating, and I just couldn't fight it anymore. I thought, "This is my *real* home. Why am I trying to create an artificial environment for Nicky? This is how I really live. Why am I trying to raise a boy in a plastic bubble?"

I myself came from a very loud, wild, and outspoken family. Our house always had lots of visitors and constant activity. We had a dancing school in our garage, a part-time beauty salon in the kitchen, and art classes going on upstairs. And my bedroom was, by far, the noisiest in the house. It had no door and was actually connected to the kitchen/beauty shop, the busiest and neon-brightest room in the house. My room growing up was the complete opposite of what I was trying to set up for Nicky. Forget about my going to bed early or having a perfectly organized, quiet environment. I had the bright kitchen light shining in my eyes and the family phone ringing in my ears at all hours of the day and night, and while people ate late-night snacks, they could look into my room and see me sleeping in my little bed. I was the original *Truman Show!*

RE-CREATING THE WOMB

Thanks to a lot of good advice from Dr. Sharon, I've given up the notion of creating a perfect environment. I'm letting my kids see not only who *I* am, the *real* me, but also a little bit of the heritage that they came from . . . a loud and colorful family that was far from perfect. And I feel they will be much better off as human beings because they will be better able to adapt to a variety of situations and people as they move through their lives. Besides, who wants what can never be re-created? Why set up a world for your children that will never exist in the *real* world?

Dr. Sharon's View

The incredible moment of birth is, from the newborn's point of view, a rude awakening. Birth is his first encounter with frustration. Forced from the perfect environment of the womb where all his needs—nourishment, warmth, comfort, closeness, security—were met, the newborn enters a world where total gratification is no longer guaranteed. He begins to have to figure out how to get these most basic needs met within a reasonable amount of time. And from that moment on, life becomes a progression of steps moving from total dependence to self-sufficiency.

I believe that the parent who hovers over his baby, instantly gratifying every demand and avoiding the slightest frustration, denies the baby the opportunity to begin the wondrous journey of emotional development that will lead to healthy independence and self-sufficiency. Treating a baby as if he were still in the womb does a great disservice to the small but intrepid explorer who is ready and eager to take his first emotional steps in a noisy, imperfect, glorious world.

Overgratification takes many forms and often begins in the first few months of life. And ironically, what seems to a new parent like an enlightened idea or loving gesture can be anything but. One example is the entire category of products intended to simulate the experience of being in the womb. Bassinets that rock and hum, temperature-controlled cribs with vibrating mattresses, stuffed teddy bears that come with a mechanical heartbeat, all send the message that returning to the womb is desirable, thereby delaying the necessary adjustment to life outside the womb.

It isn't just products, it's parenting. The baby who is fed whether he's hungry or not is thwarted from learning to recognize hunger pangs and doesn't have an opportunity to express his needs. The baby who is picked up the minute he makes a sound is deprived of learning to tolerate frustration. Indeed, the most overgratified babies tend to grow into the most demanding, difficult children. The mother who anticipates her baby's needs before he even recognizes them slows down his emotional development. It wouldn't be surprising for this baby to grow into the kind of person who expects the world to read his mind.

There's one other common way that parents overgratify their babies (and almost never know they're doing it). And that's speaking only in soft, hushed tones. Parents who, as children, grew up with lots of yelling and screaming in their home often make a conscious decision never to raise their voices in front of *their* children. But speaking this way paints an unrealistic picture of the way the world really converses. It contributes to a child's later inability to tolerate dissension and conflict. However, as with everything else, there needs to be a balance. Abusive arguing and fighting is, in its own way, as detrimental as speaking in hushed tones.

*F*riends of mine observed a rather unusual tradition every time a new child was born into their family. After they would bring each child home from the hospital, the entire family would not leave their home or allow visitors for forty days and forty nights. Friends were told, "Please don't even call the house so that we won't be disturbed while we are bonding with our new baby." They did not want the new addition exposed to anyone outside their family circle.

On the forty-first day they would throw an enormous party so that all of their friends could meet the new arrival. Each time I went to one of these gatherings, I would observe the infant as nervous and shaky, and the other children as clingy and shy.

Now I know why.

—*Marila*

What kind of nurturing and positive encouragement contributes to a baby seeing the world as a challenging and exciting place? Watch him carefully and observe that he is naturally fascinated with the visual and auditory stimulation of his environment. Playing alone helps him develop self-sufficiency and tap inner resources. So instead of rushing "to the rescue" to entertain a baby who is playing alone, let him entertain himself. When he finally becomes bored, instead of just amusing him, read to him, sing to him, recite poetry, point to the alphabet and to numbers. Expose him to classical music from day one to help him learn to love music. In short, give him a range of great stimuli in his formative years.

BRAT-BUSTERS!

Adjusting to Sounds

We live in a small New York apartment and our baby's crib is off the dining alcove, where we both watch TV and eat. I constantly ask my husband to be quiet and wait until the baby is awake before turning on the television. He thinks the baby should get used to the noise. I think he's being insensitive. What do you think?

Dr. Sharon: From the moment of birth, a baby needs to experience the sounds of the world. Silently tiptoeing around creates an artificial environment. Television and garbage trucks are part of life. Furthermore, not to be harsh, but a baby has to discover that the world was not created just to suit him. *He* has to adjust to the world. You cannot insulate him. Turn on the television—he'll probably react much better than you think.

Marilu: This reminds me so much of my brother Lorin (the baby of the family), who is now forty years old. He cannot tolerate external noises or discomforts while he is sleeping, such as drafts, the sun rising, birds chirping, or dogs barking. He has a shag carpet draped over his bedroom window and sleeps under a deluxe electric blanket accompanied by a $200 sound machine from Brookstone that simulates Victoria Falls during the rainy season. The only thing missing from this enormous "artificial womb" is some kind of tubular attachment to the refrigerator for overnight feedings. Unfortunately for him, Hammacher-Schlemmer hasn't perfected that yet. I'm not sure, but I suspect that his oversensitivity might have something to do with the fact that when he was a baby, we older kids were forbidden even to whisper while he was sleeping. Our telephone was perpetually buried beneath three or four winter parkas until he was about fourteen. I love my brother dearly now, but back then, we all secretly wanted my mother to put him up for adoption.

When Barking Is Scary

My family doesn't have any pets because my husband is highly allergic. Consequently, my three-month-old baby is not used to animals. Every time our next-door neighbor's dog barks (a lot!), he startles and starts to cry. No matter how much I reassure him that it's okay, he's inconsolable. My husband insists that we tell the neighbors they have to control their dog. I think our baby will eventually get used to it. Help!

Dr. Sharon: Your baby's reaction is normal—the dog's barking *can be* scary. But what seems to be causing his crying is, in part, how you and your husband are reacting. If the two of you would just sit back when the dog barks and continue doing what you were doing, your baby would have (after a few incidents!) the same relaxed attitude you do. The sounds of the world—from barking dogs to loud televisions—are something a baby has to get adjusted to. And he will, with the right cues from you and your husband.

Marilu: On the second floor of my family home lived my uncle with ten cats, two dogs, two birds, a skunk, 150 fish, and his friend Charles. You can't imagine the sounds we grew up with.

Carrying a Fussy Baby

My three-month-old daughter is a fussy baby and cries a lot during the day. At first I thought she was hungry, but feeding her doesn't always work. The only time she really quiets down is when I carry her around with me. How do I break her of this? Or should I just give in and carry her everywhere in a Snugli?

Dr. Sharon: It is possible that she is colicky or allergic to formula or breast milk, so check with your pediatrician. But it's more likely that, if she's been overindulged, your three-month-old baby already has expectations and even demands. The best solution would be to hold her several times a day for ten or fifteen minutes, then put her down. If she cries, try to tolerate it. It's much harder to break habits than it is to head them off in the first place!

Marilu: It will be much easier to break her of this habit now, since she is only three months old, than it will be at three *years* old. Be grateful that you have the opportunity to correct this so early in her life. Every baby I've seen who was carried all the time seems to become not only dependent, but rather shy and incapable of being separated from his mom. The other day I was at a birthday party, and my girlfriend was there with her seven-month-old, who was never out of my friend's arms. The baby wanted nothing to do with the other children, and she wouldn't let another mother hold her. My friend feels her daughter is already too clingy, but doesn't want to go through the drama of breaking her of her habit. In your case, it may take a few days but in the long run it will be worth it.

Only Mommy

Our six-month-old son wants to be held only by me. When someone else tries to pick him up he cries. My first instinct is to let him cry, but then I feel guilty, and I reach for him. What should I be doing?

Dr. Sharon: Mothers are naturally number one in their babies' lives. If at six months your son wants to be held only by you, go along with his need. Other family members should just refrain from picking him up. That being said, it would have been best if your baby had been held by other people from day one.

Marilu: It seems to me that the sooner a mom tries to allow her child to explore other people, the better. I know it can be traumatic to force a child to be held by someone he doesn't want to be with, so of course it's important to use good judgment here. One method that might work well is for the new person to hold the baby so that he always sees you. That way he will know you are around. Gradually, as your son gets comfortable with someone you trust, you can leave the room and have some time alone.

Falling Asleep on His Own

Is it better to put a four-month-old baby in his crib awake so he can learn to fall asleep on his own, or is it okay to let him fall asleep and then put him down?

Dr. Sharon: It's much better to put the baby to bed awake so he can learn to go to sleep by himself. Falling asleep in your arms and then being placed in his crib spares him the slight healthy frustration that will help him adapt to the real world. It's a question of striking the right balance between comfort and too much comfort. However, from the very beginning, *you* will have to learn to tolerate *your* pain and anxiety at hearing your child cry for five or ten minutes as he is put down. Be sure he is dry, warm, well-fed. Then both you and your baby will simultaneously need to deal with this frustration. Once you start the habit of his falling asleep in your arms, it's going to take fifteen minutes of his unhappiness (several nights in a row) to break him of this habit.

Marilu: It is often said that you make your mistakes on the first child. Boy, did I make a mistake with Nicky when it came to putting him to bed. He wanted to be rocked to sleep while I sang to him. It was great because I got a chance to sing the hits of Broadway every night, and now Nicky is on his way to becoming the next Andrew Lloyd Webber. But it was too exhausting. With my second son, Joey, I just put him down awake and then let him learn to fall asleep on his own. To this day, he's a great sleeper.

Bedtime Rituals

I've developed a very successful ritual for putting my five-month-old baby to sleep. I give her a bath, give her a nighttime feeding, place her in her crib with a night-light on, and put on a nursery tape. At the end of the tape, I turn out the light and kiss her good night and close the door. A couple of nights ago as I put her to bed, I put on her tape and the batteries ran out. Without her music, she couldn't get to sleep. I realized that she's way too dependent on this ritual. Should I try to vary this ritual so she becomes more flexible? Or should I keep doing what's she's used to and what usually works just fine?

Dr. Sharon: The items (like blankets and stuffed animals) and the rituals that babies become deeply attached to, particularly at bedtime, are the equivalent of emotional medicine to them. The same way you wouldn't forget your baby's medicine, just make sure you have a spare set of batteries in the house! In time, on her own, your baby will outgrow these rituals.

Marilu: I remember when Nicky was two months old his favorite thing to look at was a black-and-white bull's-eye card. It would entertain him during diaper changing or calm him down when he got overtired. We carried it with us everywhere and one time left it behind at friends'. I actually had a messenger pick it up and deliver it. (Talk about overindulgence!) Nicky enjoyed the card that evening, but within a week had moved on to trapezoids.

Relatives Roughhousing

My sister and her husband are my baby's closest family. As much as I love my brother-in-law, he has no instinct for babies. He treats my seven-month-old boy like a football, tossing him in the air and pretending (for fun!) to drop him. When I tell him he's scaring the baby, he laughs it off. Am I being too overprotective?

Dr. Sharon: Unless your baby is fearful and crying, you shouldn't automatically assume that your brother-in-law is scaring him. What should scare you is that your baby's neck is not being supported when he's tossed in the air. Make sure he is always held in ways that are safe.

Marilu: If you love your brother-in-law, then you should feel comfortable expressing your concerns and he should respect that. Tell him to postpone the football game at least until your boy is in Pull-Ups.

Working Mom Wants to Stay in Touch

I'm a working mother who travels a lot. Someone suggested I line pictures of myself around the crib when I'm on a business trip. Do you think this makes sense?

Dr. Sharon: Oddly enough, lining the crib with your pictures may have a negative effect on your baby, only reminding him that you are gone. He will not be comforted. His birth experience initiated him to the physical and emotional pain of separation. Having survived that, he can contend with your short business trip.

One more caveat: If pictures are unnecessary, recording your voice for the baby to listen to in your absence is equally unhelpful. It serves only to remind the baby that the parent is not physically there with him.

Marilu: Lining the crib with photos sounds a bit narcissistic. I have found that the best way to keep my boys happy and content while I'm away is to show them continuous reruns of *Taxi.* (I'm just kidding.)

Fear of the Pediatrician

My four-month-old daughter is afraid of our pediatrician. This pediatrician has taken care of our six-year-old son since he was born and our son is very fond of him. Should I get a different pediatrician for our daughter? One that would be a better match with her personality?

Dr. Sharon: At four months, it's natural for your daughter to be afraid of a doctor. However well-intentioned, it would be wrong for you to change pediatricians on the basis of her age-appropriate fears. Your six-year-old son is attesting to the fact that the pediatrician is okay. Plus, you're there when your daughter is being examined so you could tell if the pediatrician were being too harsh with her. Since that's not the case, stick with the pediatrician and don't let your daughter run the show.

Marilu: The most important thing to remember when dealing with a pediatrician (or any doctor, for that matter) is that you must work *with* him to get the best results. It's teamwork. Know as much as you can about your family's history and trust your instincts as a parent. Don't be afraid to ask questions and educate yourself so that you always know what your doctor is talking about.

Breast-Feeding Isolation

I am a breast-feeding mother of a newborn. I love breast-feeding and I'm committed to feeding on demand. But it makes me terribly self-conscious to breast-feed in front of anyone other than my husband. Consequently, I'm feeling very isolated. I don't have people over and I don't go out much. I don't have enough milk to pump. Do you think I should give up nursing?

Dr. Sharon: Being self-conscious about breast-feeding in public is a statement about your modesty, which is an admirable trait. More important, I am a big proponent of feeding on demand (just make sure your baby is only fed when he is really hungry and doesn't get into the habit of using your breast as a pacifier). However, since you say you don't have much milk, teach your baby to get a bottle of formula occasionally. That way you don't have to give up something that means so much to you and your baby. Breast-feed your baby at home, then go out on short excursions where you can see friends and feel more connected, or take a bottle of formula with you so you can spend more quality time with your friends.

Marilu: If your milk supply is low, the best way to increase it is to drink more water (and nonalcoholic beer, too!). Eat more protein and mochi (a brown rice product found in health food stores). Breast-feeding and pumping have a demand-and-supply relationship. If you pump after you breast-feed, you will also eventually increase your milk supply. Try to be patient. It may take a while to see the results. Recent studies have shown that if you can breast-feed your baby for a year, the rewards will be great because your child will be so much healthier.

WHEN LITTLE BRATS BECOME BIG BRATS

We've already learned that finding a balance between frustration and gratification starts from day one, but what happens when the twenty-four-hour womb service continues throughout a child's life?

Dr. Sharon's View

At nine months, Jared tries to reach for the toy on top of the table. "Oh, no, Jared," says his mother, pained at his effort, "let me get that." At two years, Jared tries to hang his jacket up all by himself. "That's too hard for you, sweetie," says his loving mother, "let me help." At six years, Jared slowly signs his name with his favorite crayon to a drawing he has just finished, but as he tries to get it straight, his mother prints it neatly for him. "See, Jared, that's how you do it. Isn't that better?" At every stage, Jared's mother only wants to help. But every time she helps, Jared feels certain that he must be helpless, otherwise why would his mother keep interfering? With every passing year, Jared feels closer than ever to—and more dependent on—his mother.

Having been shielded from frustration, challenges, and painful experiences in childhood, the adult lives not in the real world, but in a kind of cocoon. He is, in essence, an infant in an adult body. Not equipped to overcome problems, he grows up limited both in his personal relationships and in relating to his peers, still hoping that his needs will be anticipated and met. He says "I can't" with great frequency. In fact, the dependency fostered by overindulgence is one of the most important themes of this book, because it is so crucial to determining a child's growth and potential.

Perhaps the greatest tragedy of childhood overgratification is that its damage in adulthood is extremely difficult, if not impossible, to reverse. Laying down the law—"either get a job or get out"—may cause the dependent adult to become further nonfunctioning, slumping into a depression. It's too late to give ultimatums. The problem was not created just by telling the child that he was "special"—*it was created by a lack of demands, expectations, and boundaries.*

And there is one more sad legacy. The adult who was given twenty-four-hour womb service when he was growing up, excessively pampered and indulged, will *not,* quite surprisingly, recall any of this fondly. Indeed, he will honestly recall his childhood as a miserable time and blame his parents for mistreating him, when in fact they did quite the opposite. This is a very important eye-opener for adults who carry lifelong grudges against their parents. There is hope for these adults once they understand this surprising concept of their upbringing, and start to deal with the long-lasting damage that overindulgence created for them.

CHAPTER 2

Independence 101

I've always been fascinated by the process of learning. What seems at first to be overwhelming and frustrating (learning to crawl, walk, talk, read, dress, ride a bike, and so on) soon becomes second nature, and we can barely remember those first moments when we felt overchallenged. We tend to associate learning with starting school, but learning begins the day we are born. I was lucky enough to have two older sisters (four and a half and nine years older) who loved to play teacher with me. Along with school-type lessons, like reading and writing, they taught me practical lessons like crawling, using a glass instead of a bottle, brushing my teeth, and tying my shoes. By the time I started kindergarten, they had already exposed me to many of the lessons they had learned, so I felt well-prepared for school from the very beginning. I wanted to provide the same learning environment for my sons when they were born.

One of the most valuable lessons I've learned over the years (sometimes the hard way) is that the best way to teach someone is to let him do it himself. I always keep that in mind when teaching my boys. For example, for Nicky's first lesson on day one, I put him on his stomach so that he would naturally want to push up. This can be frustrating for a baby, especially a one-day-old, but it is a wonderful exercise because it gradually develops his arms, which is necessary for him to begin crawling, which leads to walking, which leads to exploring, which leads to independence. The basic idea is that it is best to let babies and children do as much for themselves as possible. At first, when I put Nicky on his stomach, he really didn't like it. When his arms got stronger, though, he stopped disliking it and was actually proud of himself. Next, I started placing desirable objects, like a set of keys out of reach in front of him, so he would be motivated to reach for it. I let him get it sometimes, but, most of the time, I would place the object farther and farther away, which would frustrate him even more. My friends would say, "You're terrible!" or "How can you frustrate him like that?" But that struggle was just what he needed to learn eventually to crawl. It was a very exciting day when he finally made that breakthrough. His efforts reminded me of what I used to go through as a dancer when I would work through a new dance step that I couldn't get right away. I would practice and practice, and then, all of a sudden, the muscle memory would take over my body and I would nail the step. I thought of this as I watched Nicky reach his moment of accomplishment, first going right, and then moving left, and recognizing that this was getting him closer to the keys. To this day, he approaches learning something new with the same technique, understanding that once he can break through the frustration of repetition, he will accomplish a new goal.

WHEN YOU PREVENT
A CHILD FROM MOVING ON

As I said earlier, the key to teaching your children is to let them do as many things as possible by themselves. Through Dr. Sharon, I've learned that there are two main problems that we as parents run into with this directive. First, many parents hate to see their kids struggle and be frustrated, even for a moment, so they jump in and help after they detect the slightest amount of discomfort. One of the worst things we can do as parents is to hold our children back from the progress that they want to make themselves. The second problem is the time factor. It's often necessary for us to move quickly through our lives, so we expect these little people to work at our pace with the expediency of a grown-up. Because it's so easy just to cruise through our lives with the speed and ease we're used to as adults, we usually take that easier and faster route. But it's important to take the time to let our children dress themselves, feed themselves, struggle on the floor when they're learning to crawl, or walk slowly when they're learning to walk. It's so much easier, and takes so much less time, for us just to pick up the baby and go. I used to pride myself on the fact that I could get both kids dressed and out the door in record time. Now I force myself to let them gather their things, dress themselves, and put on their own shoes. All I can say is . . . thank God for Velcro!

Here's what Dr. Sharon has to say on the subject.

Dr. Sharon's View

A baby tries to reach for something, he struggles, he has difficulty getting hold of it, he keeps trying, he's still trying his hardest . . . but his mother, watching this, hands it to him. And while she gives the now-smiling baby the object that he wants, what she is taking away from him is much more significant. She is unconsciously taking away her child's emotional and physical muscles, undermining his first brave efforts to become self-resourceful and independent.

The child who fends for himself thinks, "Oh, great! Mommy and Daddy think I can do it. I've got my own arms and legs and brains and my own ability. I *can* do it." And this is the beginning of a highly functioning, independent individual. This is a child who learns and grows with each small challenge he faces. But the parent who cannot tolerate seeing the baby struggle, who believes him to be helpless, will produce a child who *is* helpless, a child who forever wants a parent to help with every task. Interestingly, the parent who has the hardest time watching his child struggling with frustration was probably overgratified himself when he was growing up. His child's struggle will remind him, in painful ways, of his own low frustration tolerance. Occasionally the parent who was neglected will want to give his child a better experience and will err in the same way as the parent who was overindulged.

Not letting a child move forward starts from the very beginning of life. The baby who is given a bottle when he can (and given a choice, *would*) drink from a glass, or the toddler who is carried when he can walk, gets the message that to grow up and fend for himself is not desirable. He suspects that he needs a lot of help. When a parent becomes the child's arms, legs, and brains, that child's independence and self-sufficiency are thwarted. The result? A child who is unequipped to deal with the pitfalls of life. A child who is likely to become bewildered and even resentful of demands made of him.

To what extent the damage of overgratification can be fully undone depends on when parents stop the overindulgence. If the child is two years old when the indulgence stops, the chances of damage being reversed are good. If the child is five and already has trouble in school, it is difficult but not impossible. It takes effort and determination for parents to change their approach and not waver. Once the child has reached his teens the damage is difficult to reverse, but can to some extent be repaired. If a child has been overindulged into the teens, precautions must be taken when making an attempt to put an end to the overgratification. It is unwise to insist that a teenager "shape up" when his "emotional wings" have been clipped by doing too much for him as he grew up. But the lucky child whose parents understand the importance of providing a balance of frustration and gratification will thrive, developing a great capacity for overcoming adversity throughout life.

Pampering a Sick Child

Even parents who watch their child confront a new task or challenge without interfering or "helping" have a hard time maintaining that admirable independent stance when their child is sick. Of course, it probably goes without saying that it's imperative for parents to make sure their sick child's basic needs are well taken care of; that the child is properly medicated, properly nourished, warm, and resting comfortably. But hovering over a child who's in bed with a head cold or flu, overreacting at the first sneeze, ministering to him with extraordinary attention and sympathy, only gives the child the impression that there are tremendous emotional rewards attached to being sick.

At the risk of making a generalization, children who are showered with attention when they are sick tend to lack resilience in other areas of their lives. They are often the children who take the longest time to recover from emotional wounds, blowing up minor insults and experiencing them as irreparable hurts or treating everyday problems as if they were dire emergencies. This kind of distorted thinking can lead to great unhappiness as well as some serious errors in judgment later on.

When I was in my early twenties, my boyfriend at the time expected me to wait on him hand and foot when he got sick. He would use a mild cold as an excuse to stay home and away from responsibility for a whole week. I would fluff up his pillows, bring him chicken soup, and make sure he had the right amount of magazines and the TV remote control nearby. It was just so ridiculous and seemed so counterproductive to getting well. He told me stories about how his mother overpampered him when he was sick as a child. He simply *loved* being sick.

I grew up in a household where my father would often say, "People should be blamed for their sicknesses, not pitied." So we rarely acted like we were sick. In fact, he would also say, "Why do you want to stay home when you're sick? You should go to school when you're sick and take off on a day that you're healthy." He felt you shouldn't waste a free day being sick.

I remember one rare exception when I was overpampered. I was sick when I was ten years old and had a violent allergic reaction to the penicillin I was given. My recovery took over two weeks. I got extremely attached to my mother during that period, because I was home with her for so long. But it wasn't because she indulged me in the usual way, in fact, quite the contrary. I barely saw her during the day while she did beauty work and taught dancing. But at night, I stayed up with her watching *The Late Show* and *The Late-Late Show* until four o'clock in the morning.

That bonded us forever. So it wasn't that she brought me too many cookies and milk in bed, or whatever. It had more to do with living like a grown-up for the two and a half weeks that made me want to get sick more often.

— *Marilu*

BRAT-BUSTERS!

When to Stop Breast-Feeding

I am still breast-feeding my three-year-old son and being criticized by my family. They say it isn't healthy for a boy who is already walking and talking and even toilet-trained. Please advise.

Dr. Sharon: Since your son has already successfully dealt with the frustrations of toilet-training and learning to talk, breast-feeding now is a form of overgratification. There's another reason to stop. If it is your husband who is critical of this, there is a good chance he will come to resent your son's relationship with you.

Marilu: I am a big advocate of breast-feeding. I breast-fed both of my sons for a year. In fact, I have an award from the La Leche League for the work I've done campaigning for breast-feeding. It was one of the greatest experiences of my life, but when it was time to wean them, as emotional as it was for me, I felt it was important to let them move on to the next phase. If your son is capable of talking and using the toilet by himself, he is certainly capable of using a cup. Put it this way, any child who can ask for it by name should no longer be breast-feeding. If he is saying things like, "Okay, let me move to the right one now," you've probably let him go way too long!

Eating with His Fingers

Should I spoon-feed my fourteen-month-old or let him eat with his fingers?

Dr. Sharon: Letting him feed himself is a good way to encourage your fourteen-month-old's independence. And if he's not interested in eating at one meal, he'll probably get the nourishment he needs in the course of the day at other meals. Check with your pediatrician if you have any concerns.

Marilu: Once kids start eating, it's better to let them feed themselves because it's important for them to establish their own rhythms of eating. So many adults are obese because they were overfed as children and not allowed to listen to their own bodies' needs. As messy as it is sometimes, children need to develop their own relationship with food based on their internal signals rather than the timing and volume control assumed by an adult.

A Child's Lack of Fear Can Be Scary

My fifteen-month-old has no fear of danger and often takes risks. I think he'd go out the window and try to fly if I didn't watch his every move. How can I teach him about danger?

Dr. Sharon: Almost every move a baby makes has some risk factor since he is so young and not yet coordinated. So you do have to stay ever-vigilant about keeping him from a potentially dangerous situation. But just as psychologically dangerous would be if you were so worried about your son's safety that you didn't encourage him to explore the world on his own.

Marilu: My Joey is a born daredevil. The first time I took him to a kids' gym, at seventeen months, he jumped into the "ball crawl" like he was a salmon spawning. I'm grateful he's more cautious now, but he learned the hard way. He had already been to the emergency room four times for daredevil-type things by the time he was two and a half. Actually, I'm getting a little dramatic here. The worst thing he ever did was crash his tricycle into a tree after rolling down a hill. I'm giving the impression that he's out skydiving and bungee jumping. I won't allow that until he's at least four.

Skipping Grades

I have a real dilemma on my hands. My daughter has just completed her kindergarten year. Her teacher and the principal of the school are recommending that she skip to second grade. She is already a fluid reader and understands the basic principles of math. The school feels first grade would not be challenging as she is exceptionally bright and hungry to learn. I am reluctant because she is so happy with her classmates, and an enormous part of school for her is friends. The school made it clear that it will support any choice I make on her behalf. Should I keep her where she is or have her begin second grade in the fall?

Dr. Sharon: You have two choices—keep her in first grade and provide her with challenging educational materials and books after school, or have her skip to second grade and have friends her age come over after school. There's no reason you can't ask her for her preference. You can simply state that she would learn more if she skips first grade and she would still get to see her friends after school. It depends on the child. Some children can absorb a tremendous amount of information at this age but are too immature to jump a grade. Also, give thought to getting professional help in assessing your child's readiness (her ability to keep up academically as well as her emotional and physical maturity).

Marilu: When I was your daughter's age, it was recommended that I skip first grade, too. My mom was a firm believer that it was better to stay with friends my own age than to skip a grade. Her opinion was based more on a "big fish, little pond" theory, but I'll never know whether or not she was right. All I can tell you is that I loved school, graduated first in my grammar school and third in my high school, and challenged myself after and outside school with extracurricular activities.

Alone in a Public Place

Last Saturday I took my nine-year-old son and four-year-old daughter to see a movie. They were excited and I was thrilled to find one that they'd both like. In the middle of the movie, my daughter had to go to the bathroom, and I told my son he had to come with us and wait outside the ladies' room. He said, "No, Mom, I'll stay right here. I promise I won't go anywhere." I didn't feel comfortable leaving him there by himself but I also felt bad about interrupting his movie. Did I do the right thing?

Dr. Sharon: Leaving your nine-year-old son in the theater unattended would have been reckless. Next time, it might be a good idea to bring another adult to the movies or take your children one at a time.

Marilu: Because we live in a big city, I know I would have done the same thing. It's a shame we have to worry about things like that nowadays, but we do. Maybe next time you can bring a few of your son's friends along so that there will be more of them.

Going Alone: New Experiences

My daughter, who is nine, is really interested in art classes. I read her the brochures about all the painting, sculpting, and pottery classes. She seemed really excited, but when I went to enroll her she said she'd only go if a friend went with her. I reassured her that she would make new friends there. None of her current friends is as interested in art as she is. I think she should go by herself and take a chance, but she won't budge. Is it that she isn't open to new experiences? Help!

Dr. Sharon: It is not clear what your daughter's problem is, aside from feeling insecure by herself. At any rate, she is coming up with a simple and reasonable solution: namely, get one of her friends to join the art class with her. Such standoffs could have been avoided before your daughter began running the show. Now it's too late.

Marilu: Your daughter may also need a friend because she's talented in art and may feel more comfortable showing off in front of someone she knows. I have a friend whose son is an athlete and he often wants a friend along because, being the new guy and alone, it takes him a while to strut his stuff.

Sleeping Away from Home

My daughter is ten. Almost all her friends are going to sleep-away camp or going to stay with grandparents for a week in another city, and so on. My daughter doesn't want to sleep away from home for even one night. Her summer seems to be lonely but she would rather be alone than away from home. Should we force her?

Dr. Sharon: Forced separation is generally not a good idea. There could be any number of reasons your daughter is opposed to staying away from home, among them fear of missing something good during her absence. Or it could be a more anxiety-producing reason: She could feel insecure about being away from you, fearing you might get ill. Fear of separation needs to be respected. Let her decide when she's comfortable being away by herself.

Marilu: Your daughter would have loved my mom's rule. We weren't allowed to spend the night away from home until we were twelve. My mother would let anyone stay at our house (the more, the merrier), but when it came to her kids, she wanted us home. Looking back, I'm sure that she didn't want to miss us.

Creative Freedom

My six-year-old daughter received a paint-by-number game for her birthday. She used to draw pictures and paint her own paintings but now she meticulously fills in little spaces with predetermined colors. What do you think of this activity?

Dr. Sharon: Paint-by-number canvases are confining and don't allow for creativity. Coloring books aren't much better. It's best to give a child large sheets of paper, watercolors, brushes, and lots of space to work freely. Don't suggest what he should paint or volunteer your interpretation of his work. Say "good job" and hang up one of his paintings every once in a while.

Marilu: Everyone in my family is artistic except me, and I think it's because I got so obsessed with those paint-by-number kits. It was more important for me to fill in the spaces inside the lines perfectly and with the right colors than to look at the big picture and think in terms of creating my own work. I'm great at filling in spaces. No one can touch me when it comes to Tetris. But I'm a terrible artist. And I blame paint-by-number. I would like to gather all the inartistic people in this country and start a class action suit against Hasbro. I'll set up a test on my Web site. Please contact me if you can't draw "Binky."

Coming Down with "Mommyitis"

I am lucky enough to have wonderful full-time help. My son is in nursery school in the mornings five days a week. Since his first school experience means exposure to more germs, he has come down with the usual kid fevers and infections. When he is home from school with a fever, I feel his "mommyitis" is justified. I want to take off work to be with him. I know by staying with our housekeeper, he is in good, loving hands, but isn't it true that you just want your mommy when you're sick?

Dr. Sharon: You sound like a good, sympathetic mother and it's hard not to feel sympathetic when your child wants you. However, what your child wants isn't necessarily in his best interest. Babying your son when he is sick sends the wrong message and creates a destructive bonding between the two of you. Since he is in good, loving hands, stay at work and let him be cared for by your housekeeper.

Marilu: Oh boy, this is a tough one. Kids are never more vulnerable than when they're sick, and I know from my own experience that nothing pulls on your heart strings more than a fevered, jammied, little bundle of need who wants to be cozied. But let's think this through. If you indulge him and stay home, your son may enjoy being with you so much that he will learn how to fake or exaggerate sickness in the future just to be with you. Remember your own childhood—we've all tried the old thermometer on the radiator trick at least once.

WHEN LITTLE BRATS
BECOME BIG BRATS

As you can see, our job as parents is all about giving children the tools they need to learn, grow, and cope in the outside world while trying to avoid the temptation of doing too many things for them (even though those things may seem unimportant and harmless). Here's what can happen to children who grow up overpampered and deprived of learning simple skills:

Dr. Sharon's View

Running on the playground, Cora and Gerry bumped into each other and both fell. Cora's mother scurried over, gasping loudly, "Oh no, are you okay, darling? It's okay!" as she picked up and enveloped her sobbing, inconsolable three-year-old. Gerry's mother, on the other hand, witnessing the same collision take place, stood up and called "Safe!" from a distance as Gerry "slid into home base," then got up, brushed himself off, and announced, "I'm okay." Gerry ran off to play with some other kids, while Cora's mother had to take her home.

Cora, of course, didn't mind, since she has a playmate who does not leave her side. Her name is Mommy and she takes up most of the room in the sandbox, to the dismay of the other kids whose faces turn long when she takes off her pumps and sits cross-legged next to her daughter, spooning sand into a bucket. Cora follows her mother everywhere, becoming depressed when she is out of sight. Cora's behavior is easily explained by her mother's behavior. Since Cora was a baby, she had been at Cora's beck and call day and night. Cora is now a helpless child who needs her mother near her at all times.

The child whose parents anticipated his needs, thereby undervaluing his strengths and skills, will never fully use his talents when he grows up. The child whose parents *overvalued* his abilities by praising him unstintingly will also suffer adult consequences. He will feel a false sense of entitlement, constantly needing compliments for each and every small accomplishment and will have trouble creating and maintaining good relationships.

The child whose worried parents hovered over him when he was sick will, as an adult, seek an overwhelming display of concern and attention from his spouse and his friends. He might live in a state of anxiety. Never feeling really healthy, he will expect sympathy even when he isn't sick at all.

The overtended and overindulged child is not equipped to understand his role in assuming responsibilities for himself as he grows up. The anxiety he lives with is an expression of concern about how to deal with life's daily, as well as long-term, demands. Clearly, then, parents will be helping their children become secure and confident adults by fostering their independence from an early age.

CHAPTER 3

"No Screaming, No Biting, No Dairy Products, No Sugar"

$\mathcal{B}$eing an actress, I know what contracts are, and I never start work until everything between my new employer and me is agreed upon, and both parties have signed on the dotted line. We all understand what a paper contract is, but do you realize that, as Dr. Sharon explains it, we have a contract with each and every person in our lives? From our most personal relationships to the people with whom we have the briefest, most perfunctory association, there is always an unspoken mutually agreed upon contract as to how each of us is to handle ourselves in that exchange or relationship.

For example, if you are in a restaurant and a waitress does a particularly good job, the contract is that you, the patron, leave a nice tip. You would be in violation of that unspoken contract if you chose instead to hug and kiss her to express your gratitude. When you call Information for a telephone number, it would be a violation of the basic contract that you have with the operator (a total stranger) to discuss anything other than the information she needs to perform her job and supply you with the telephone number or address you requested. In public, it is most generally accepted that we will be properly clothed and will refrain from touching one another. If someone bumps you in a crowd, don't you immediately recoil in defense? When a person on the street solicits you for money and follows you, don't you feel awkward and uncomfortable? In overcrowded situations, physical fights will actually break out because there is an unspoken agreement that we all travel with a certain amount of space around us which is ours, and that contract should not be violated.

These same principles apply to our own families' contracts, albeit with broader boundaries and greater intimacy. In my family, we had an unspoken agreement that no one (especially my parents) would parade around naked or inappropriately dressed (although my mother rarely wore anything other than a leotard or a bathing suit). When I was growing up, there were some funny rules between my mother and us kids, the most important being we couldn't wake her before noon unless we brought her a . . . Pepsi. For instance, whenever I needed a dollar for school, I would cautiously knock (Pepsi in hand) and wait to be called into her darkened room. She would sit up groggily, take a swig, and then tell me to get her purse. But God forbid I should ever open her purse myself. That was another contract. The only person allowed into the inner sanctum of my mother's hallowed purse was my mother.

My father's contract, on the other hand, was simple—"Listen to your mother!" The only other rule was that we all had to help him clean the house on Wednesdays, his day off and our only precious half-day off from school. He would don his sporty Robert Hall gray-and-white speckled shirt, the only thing in his closet that wasn't a suit (my father ran an automobile dealership), and we all knew it was time to get busy. My parents rarely had to spell out the contract. We just knew.

Although I am very different from my parents (times have changed), I have come to realize that my sons also understand most of our contracts without my totally spelling them out. The first time I was aware that I even had a specific contract with my boys was when I overheard Nicky, at two-and-a-half, tell one of his friends who was screaming at the time, "You can't scream. Mommy says, 'No screaming, no biting, no dairy products, no sugar!'"

THE CONTRACT BETWEEN PARENT AND CHILD

The basic contract that Rob and I have established with our boys is fairly simple: We are the parents, they are the children, they live in our home, they follow our rules. Although this sounds pretty obvious, it is actually a notion that escapes many households for a variety of reasons, such as the idea that kids' feelings should be respected to the point where the child has equal say with his parents. By having our children grasp the basic understanding of our contract, I believe we are experiencing fewer arguments, fewer tantrums, and certainly far fewer lengthy explanations. Dr. Sharon has taught us that by establishing clearly defined contracts with our children, we are trying to give them a greater sense of security, stability, and a more realistic sense of expectation. (We're trying to, anyway!)

Here's what she has to say on the subject.

Dr. Sharon's View

Corporations, marriages, trade unions—all function because of contracts they've mutually agreed on. On a smaller, but no less important level, *parents and children need to create an unwritten contract* to make the family function. This contract is: "I am the parent, I make the rules. You are the child, you obey them!"

And far from being harsh or absolute, *a parent who consistently respects and adheres to this will help promote healthy, cooperative relationships between every member of the family.* Children who respect this contract will grow up knowing their place in the family and in society. They will know what is expected of them. They will know what they can expect from their parents. They will feel secure.

But the child who controls the household (whether he takes over or the parent abdicates), ordering his parents around and monitoring, criticizing, or nagging his siblings—or the student who "takes over" the class from the teacher or who monopolizes the teacher's time, all break contracts and create confusion. When a parent or teacher permits a child to break the contract, boundaries of safety cease to exist for the child, his sense of security is undermined, and a great deal of emotional confusion can ensue.

Equally troubling is when a child entices the parent into breaking the contract, for on some level the child hopes that the parent will remain steadfast, since this contract is the foundation of the parent-child relationship. When a parent breaks the agreement, the child is likely to experience a great deal of anxiety since he will interpret his parent's action as a weakness. For instance, the child who incessantly nags his parents to let him stay up late and watch TV may wear his parents down. But once they give him permission to stay up, he will become anxious at not having his parents remain in charge and help him maintain a routine. His parents at the same time will gradually become resentful of having given him permission.

It takes a great deal of willpower for a parent to honor the contract, to be steadfast and not budge, especially in the face of a child's constant demands to the contrary. The parent must prevail, though, since it is the parent who sets the example of how other relationships remain intact. Another crucial reason for parents to uphold contracts is that children take their cues from their parents—often unconsciously. If parents break contracts, the child quickly sees that, in his own life, he has a choice to obey or not obey society's rules and laws. For instance, one contract that is frequently disregarded has to do with being punctual and respecting another person's time. A parent who promises to pick up a child at a certain time and is chronically late gives the child the message that it's okay to disregard an agreed-upon time and to make someone wait.

Children naturally imitate the positive qualities of each parent, *providing* they have not been consistently overindulged. But the overindulged child, to the parents' dismay, will imitate the negative qualities of both parents. An example of this might be a parent who is not truthful. The child, picking up on this, will later have a tendency to alter the truth himself. Uncanny as it seems (and of great surprise to Mom and Dad), children pick up their parents' behavior even if the parents keep it "secret."

Doing chores, doing homework, going to bed on time—these are the most basic contracts of childhood. But there are other understood, unspoken "contracts" with the child's environment that children begin to enter into at a very young age. They are dealing with teachers, shopkeepers, bus drivers, neighbors. Simple as they may seem, these relationships in society provide a framework for everyone's life, teaching children how to keep within the boundaries of cooperation and helping them function adeptly. Parents need to help children respect these contracts.

My father, the salesman, with his "get rich quick" schemes, figured out a great way for us to learn the value of money and at the same time honor one of my mother's most important rules of the house. No one was allowed to say "shut up," and if anyone did, they had to pay a quarter to the Family Kitty. This system became so effective my parents introduced another contract as well: If you said something bad about your brother or sister (i.e., "you're a stupid . . .") you had to pay a nickel, and if you said something about yourself ("I'm such an idiot . . .") you had to pay a quarter. This not only taught us about respect and self-esteem but eventually gave us enough money for a family vacation!

—Marla

BRAT-BUSTERS!

When Children and Parents Become Peers

My friend confides in her nine-year-old daughter about her personal problems. I think she is burdening her child. What do you think?

Dr. Sharon: I agree with you. It's destructive for a child to be burdened with the parent's problems or secrets. In a healthy family, parents and children each have a defined and different role. Contrary to popular belief, parents and children cannot (and should not) be "friends" in this sense.

Marilu: I have noticed that this is really common in divorced families. I've seen fathers who treat their teenage boys like buddies, confiding in them about their sex lives or bragging about their conquests. I've also seen divorced moms who wanted their children to know how "wronged" they were by their former husbands. I really feel that parents should be careful not to do this. It is unfair to their children and former spouses, and it definitely breaks the parent-child contract.

Grandma's Different Rules

My mother baby-sits for our children two evenings a week. I've explained to her our daily routine and method of discipline, but she refuses to follow them. She lets the children watch too much television, stay up an hour past their bedtime, and have more sweets than they are allowed. What effect will Grandma have on the children?

Dr. Sharon: Happily, your children are firmly anchored in the disciplined world since you spend much more time with them than their grandmother. You have three options: The children are told that when Grandma comes over, some of the family rules are altered. The second is to make it clear to your mother that she must follow your rules when she baby-sits. The third is not to have her baby-sit at all. If you choose the first option, accept the more liberal rules and don't make an issue of Grandma's "spoiling" the children.

Marilu: How lucky you are to have your mother help you once in a while. I always think it is so important for children to know their families. However, if you're really fighting over your opposed methods of routine and discipline, maybe you should let your mom take the kids less often, so that when she *does* take them, she can have her relationship with them. We are never going to be able to control all the people who come in contact with our children.

Family Trips

We have four children, ages five to twelve. On the weekends, every time we try to decide on an excursion, there is dissension. Should we decide our outings based on democracy and let the majority rule, or should we, as the parents, avoid the arguments and make the choice ourselves?

Dr. Sharon: Because your children's ages range so greatly, there's no wonder that they will want to do different things. Make the decision yourselves. If they are accustomed to their parents being in charge, they will cooperate and look forward to the group excursion.

Marilu: My parents usually made the decisions about what we would do, but sometimes the kids decided *where* we would do it. For example, every Wednesday, on my father's day off, we made it a point to go "out" for dinner and each kid took turns deciding where we would go. This was a great idea! We would do research to find a good restaurant because we all took pride in our own selection when our turn came up. In fact, we would then rate the restaurants on a one-to five-star system. It was our first lesson in making an informed decision and in taking responsibility for our own choices. Somehow my younger brother Lorin got four-and-a-half stars for choosing Arby's after my choice of the Travelodge coffeehouse only got four stars. And mine was "all you can eat"! Although I must admit that Arby's in the sixties was a more glamorous dining experience.

Hard Work and Privilege

Our family is affluent and we have worked hard to achieve this. We are generous with our children with respect to money and material possessions. How do we show our children a connection between hard work and privilege? We don't want them to be spoiled.

Dr. Sharon: If your children work hard at school, get good grades, go to bed on time, and do their chores when they're asked to, there's no reason for you to be concerned. Responsible children understand the contract that exists between them and their academics—they will make the connection between hard work and privilege, and your generosity will not cause them to be spoiled.

Marilu: Out here in Hollywood I've seen parents' generosity either spoil their children or inspire them to work hard and make something of themselves. It all depends on the parents' example and rules. If we have respect for money and material possessions, our children will, too.

Rewarding Good Grades

My daughter has been falling behind in her grades. I only expect her to do her best, but I believe that a lot of her Bs and Cs are because of her slacking off. Her teacher agrees that she's not working to her full aptitude. Is it a good idea for me to promise her a reward of some kind if she brings up her grades in her next report card? And if she doesn't bring up her grades, should I dock her allowance?

Dr. Sharon: There are a couple of issues here. First of all, a good grade ought to be a reward in itself. Promising an additional reward as an incentive is okay, but withholding something like an allowance is not a good idea. In this case, promising a reward is a better option than threatening a punishment. In addition, you might explain to your daughter that excellent grades now could help her get accepted into a good school later, which in turn could strongly determine her success in life.

Marilu: I think if a child expects money for good grades, she could also end up only being interested in the classes that are easy. That's not a contract you would want to uphold! School would become a moneymaking opportunity, instead of a learning one.

"But All the Other Kids Are Going!"

My eleven-year-old son was looking forward to a much anticipated sleepover party. The parents rented an R-rated movie for the children to watch. None of the other parents seemed concerned, but our rule is no R-rated movies. What do we do?

Dr. Sharon: It's so important for parents to monitor what their children watch. Since your rule is no R-rated movies, make no exceptions. Tell your son that his friend's parents' decision is unacceptable to you and violates your rules. As hard as it might be, tell him that, because of this, he is not allowed to attend the sleepover.

Marilu: When I was a child, the Catholic Church defined what movies we could see by rating them according to the Legion of Decency guidelines—A, A2, A3, B, and C for condemned. This rating system was very similar to the one we have now, but it was reinforced by our school and the church's position. That made it easier for parents to set a standard and have their children respect it. Today, the rules of the house are the rules of the house, and even though occasionally they can be broken, I really do believe that children feel more secure if these rules are defined and upheld.

What Lateness Means

My thirteen-year-old son is chronically late to every event. My husband and I find this very disruptive and rude. What makes it even more maddening is that I am always early. I'm not sure what these patterns mean or what I can do about them.

Dr. Sharon: A person who is frequently late shows contempt (without always realizing it) for the contract that demands punctuality and a regard for other people's time. Chronic lateness is a symptom of breaking the rules, which usually points to having been overgratified by one or both of his parents. Being frequently *early* is a symptom of anxiety. Unfortunately, it takes a great deal of effort to change either of these behaviors. Respect for time and punctuality are part of the foundation of one's upbringing. Encourage punctuality and forgive occasional lapses.

Marilu: Oh boy, does this sound like my family. When we were kids, every clock in our house was anywhere from five to forty minutes fast. Each room had its own time zone. If you were running late, you could always move to a room where you were early. To this day, some of the people in our family are always late. My brother Lorin's wedding started an hour and twelve minutes late. I know the precise time because my husband started a $5 pool and that was the winning time. Even some of the parish nuns, who know my family well, entered the pool. In Lorin's wedding video, the entire congregation is visibly concerned about "post time" when the kid (the ring boy) steps on the paper (the official start of the wedding). At that moment everyone looks at my husband for the official time, and then congratulates the winner, completely ignoring the wedding procession.

When to Stay Out of It

Our sixteen-year-old daughter has received three detentions last month for being late for class. She has served two detentions but forgot to attend the third. Consequently, she has now been given a *full* day—Saturday detention. She feels this is unfair and wants us to call the school to request that it be waived. What should we do?

Dr. Sharon: A full day of detention on Saturday seems severe, but for you to intervene gives her the message that she can break the rules. Stay out of it and don't share with her that you agree the punishment is unfair.

Marilu: If you get a simple traffic ticket and completely ignore it, the ticket goes to warrant and the fine multiplies from three to ten times the original cost, and in some cases, could even lead to jail time. The consequences of ignoring penalties is a good lesson for a sixteen-year-old to learn before entering the real world. (Can you tell I know someone who teaches traffic school?)

Son Taking Over the Role of Father

My husband went into a rage and moved out of the house. He lives down the street and refuses to come home. It's been about three months, and as a result, my four children are upset, especially my thirteen-year-old son, who has decided he's now the head of the house and has started bossing everyone around. Aside from the problem with my husband, what do I do about my son taking over the household?

Dr. Sharon: When a family functions properly, it is like a mobile with all the pieces hanging in balance. If one piece drops off, all the pieces must be shifted and a new balance achieved. The moment your husband moved out was the time for you to take over complete authority (which was understandably difficult during such a tumultuous time). Your son sounds like he is in a lot of pain and could use a strong parent. Start by explaining to him that you are in charge and that he must defer to you. Then investigate getting your entire family into family counseling—with such a big disruption you could all benefit.

Chores and Responsibilities

Our nine-year-old has to constantly be reminded to do his chores (setting the table at night, taking out the trash, and feeding the cat). Every day there's a battle. To solve all this fighting, what if we excused him from all chores? It would make for peace and quiet in the house.

Dr. Sharon: The child who is not asked to do any chores is overgratified. The examples you give of setting the table, taking out the trash, and feeding the cat seem reasonable chores for a nine-year-old. Maybe it's just a simple problem of forgetfulness, not inattentiveness or defiance. Some children *are* forgetful—they're not bad kids. They'll grow out of it.

Marilu: When I was a kid, my sister Christal and I were responsible for doing the dishes (a thirty-minute chore) while my brothers were responsible for taking out the garbage (a thirty-second chore). The dishes were always clean and neatly put away, while the garbage piled up like during a New York strike. Their hands were always too grubby to let them touch the dishes, but they certainly didn't get that way from touching the garbage!

WHEN LITTLE BRATS BECOME BIG BRATS

We all want our government to enforce certain rules and regulations that are meant to protect us. Even though we occasionally want to break or bend those rules (such as income tax, speeding, and so on), we are grateful and feel more secure because those rules exist. Our children, like us, really want to be protected by rules as well. As we can see, children whose parents let them manipulate contracts can grow up with a host of problems.

Dr. Sharon's View

Five-year-old Jimmy developed his own anti-parent lock system inside the car. On one side of the window was his frantic father trying to open the door. On the other side, holding down the lock, was Jimmy, with an intent look on his face. "Jimmy, it's getting late and Daddy's getting tired," Jimmy's weary father yelled through the window. Jimmy didn't budge. "You are being really bad," he said, adding, "It's past your bedtime. Stop this nonsense and come inside the house." Jimmy just looked at him. "I'll buy you that video game you wanted if you come out right now!" Jimmy could sense that his father was desperate and that the warnings would have to escalate before anything dire happened to him, so he continued bargaining. "I want the Nintendo and a Happy Meal. Besides, you're not going to bed. It's not fair," Jimmy shouted. It took fifteen minutes to get Jimmy out of the car. Once in the house, Jimmy's father gave him a lecture and Jimmy was so angry he smashed a little glass vase.

The parent-child contract was disregarded, roles were reversed, and chaos ensued. When this happens perpetually, the child grows up having little regard for the needs of others, ignoring boundaries and

lacking empathy. As an adult, he will demonstrate an inability to adhere to contracts (spoken and unspoken) within his family. He'll have problems as a spouse *and* as a parent. He may pay his bills late (or not at all). He may sleep late when he should be at work. Because he doesn't really know what a contract is, except something to scoff at or disregard, the only contract he is likely to adhere to is seeking pleasure. In extreme cases, he may not even honor the marriage contract or the law. Since there were no consequences to contend with when his parents permitted him to cajole them into breaking the contract, he believes that anything goes.

"I am the parent. I make the rules. You are the child, you obey them" is a contract that seems simple. It is not. It's difficult for the parent to adhere to, particularly because the long-term consequences of not adhering to the contract don't seem too ominous when the child is young. But knowing how devastating the effects of breaking this contract can be in the long run is a good reminder why every parent needs to be consistent and firm.

CHAPTER 4

"Wait 'Til Your Father Gets Home"

I grew up in the fifties and sixties, when most moms were home with their kids all day long. After a full day of negotiations and pleas, the only threat moms had left in their arsenal was "Wait 'til your father gets home." This, however, never worked for my mom. The problem in our house was that our father got home very late, and he didn't want to waste our precious time together by yelling at us. He was, by nature, a real jokester and entered the house like "Mr. Guest Appearance." It was like—Heeeere's Daddy!

Our mom was always trying to be serious with us and could rarely count on his support as a disciplinarian. Whenever he would scold us, it was only because our mom put him up to it, so it pretty much lost its effect. (Plus, we all knew some cute way to crack him up and lighten up the situation, if necessary.) But this was all part of their contract together as parents. It was a fairly simple contract because he was rarely home, so the two of them hardly ever clashed over how we should be raised. It was always pretty much her call.

Our family dynamic was typical for a sixties American household, but families are different now. Parents are more likely to share the duties of child rearing because it is more common for both parents to be in the workforce. And in some cases, the mother works away at an office, and the father works at home on his computer, so *he* gets to spend more time with the kids. The threat "Wait 'til your father gets home" no longer has the same impact when Dad is working in his home office or exercising down in the basement. It's hard to intimidate your kids with "Wait 'til your father gets off the Internet."

Sharing the duties of child rearing rewards parents because they work as a team to shape these precious lives. However, what if parents have opposing methods for raising their kids? Who should make all the daily decisions? Is it important to choose one parent as the "Main Boss"? Or should each parent develop independent contracts and avoid the temptation of supervising each other?

THE CONTRACT
BETWEEN PARENTS

Rob and I have learned from Dr. Sharon that couples should *not* supervise each others' parenting skills and strategies. We do our best to follow her advice, but at times this can be very difficult. Our biggest problem is that we disagree on strategies for suppressing a tantrum. Rob tends to imitate the tantrum to show them how silly it sounds, and I prefer to ignore it to show how futile it is. I believe that overpowering a tantrum is counterproductive, and he feels that ignoring it doesn't get the point across. We have always quarreled on this issue.

So, what should a couple do when their child-rearing credos clash?

Dr. Sharon's View

In the best of all worlds, parents would always agree on how to raise and discipline their children. But this is not the way the world really works. The good news is that parents with two different approaches to raising children can work well together and a child can easily adjust to their separate viewpoints. In fact, it's all for the best if a child recognizes early on that no two human beings are alike and that his parents' attitudes aren't necessarily the same. There may be conflicting opinions, but there is a simple rule of thumb that makes allowing for different parenting approaches work remarkably well: When one parent says something to the child first, the other parent then should simply abstain from giving his opinion, as hard as that might be. Privately, they agree not to interfere with each other's opinions. So there is no need to make any decisions behind closed doors. Once they decide ahead of time not to interfere, the rest is predetermined.

However, when one parent tries to supervise the other (whether it's in the presence of the child or behind closed doors), making critical comments like "I think you're too mean to Jimmy" and "Why did you put him in his room? All he said was 'I don't want to do it'" and "What's so terrible about him yelling 'no'?" the child will suffer.

There are certain extreme circumstances in which one parent *should* interfere with the other: when the child is being physically punished, inappropriately touched, or victimized by ongoing relentless derision or verbal outbursts. Under no circumstances should these kinds of violations be tolerated by the other parent.

A parent who engages in controlling or nagging or judging, or trying to will the other parent into conforming to *his* method of parenting, deprives his child of the whole rich gamut of human interactions, of exposure to divergent opinions and different ways of thinking. When the stricter of the two parents gives in and accepts the more lenient approach, the child is denied something else: the necessary discipline he thrives on. Things can be more confusing when a child is aware that one parent is critical of the other. Knowing that the lenient, permissive parent is in his corner silently (or openly) rooting for him will tend to make him uncooperative.

Interestingly, children with emotional problems, such as being overly hostile and aggressive, are rarely the result of parents who have two different approaches to child rearing.

BRAT-BUSTERS!

Let Your Husband Do It His Way

My husband teases our three-year-old daughter, imitating her crying when she's cranky and mimicking other sounds she makes. I tell him to cut it out. Should I imitate him when he's cranky to show him how obnoxious it is?

Dr. Sharon: Imitating people is hostile, so you should refrain from doing it yourself. But if that is what your husband is doing with your daughter, don't stop him. She is not being harmed and correcting his behavior is a bad idea.

Marilu: In the past, my husband tried to curtail our boys' loudness by imitating their volume, but it only made them get louder. I wanted to interfere, but I didn't because Dr. Sharon had explained it was better not to. Eventually, they all got bored with this "yelling game," especially because their audience (me) wasn't interested. The problem hardly exists now.

Should Children Interrupt Parents?

My husband frequently says "Wait a minute" to our four-year-old son, who interrupts whatever his dad is doing. I don't think it's fair. I believe that when our son interrupts his dad, one of us should pay attention to him, but my husband disagrees.

Dr. Sharon: Your husband's request to wait a minute is perfectly fine. Delayed gratification is part of the "wait a minute" request, which will help your son mature. Even if it was wrong, it makes sense for you to stay out of it.

Marilu: I think one of the best things a parent can teach a child is how to be patient.

I used to play a game with my boys when they were very little. If they wanted something (and I couldn't get it or it wasn't ready) I would say "patience," and then I would count to twenty, because that's how long it took to get them what they wanted. To this day my boys play the "patience game."

Mr. Mom

My husband is Mr. Mom, and sometimes when I come home from work, our three-year-old barely greets me, yet cries when her dad is out of sight. Since I am the breadwinner I have no choice but to work, but her reaction to me makes me miserable. What can I do?

Dr. Sharon: Could your husband and child visit you at work or meet you for lunch? Maybe on weekends, you and your daughter could spend lots of time together while your husband does the grocery shopping, and so on. As she grows up, your child will love you because of your concern for her and because you have worked to support the family, *not* because of the time you spent with her.

Marilu: Could you be acting a little guilty for going to work? Because if your daughter picks up on your dissatisfaction with the situation, she probably doesn't understand why you're not happy at home with her instead of being miserable at work. Be glad that you're such a good role model for your daughter. She'll grow up knowing a woman can be a successful mom and a successful career woman.

Good Cop/Bad Cop

My husband spends so much time at work that I have no partner in raising the children. I am the "heavy" and the "bad cop" and I resent when my husband spends a few minutes here and there having a good time with the children. Shouldn't he have to be the bad cop once in a while so the kids can see me in the same positive light that they see him?

Dr. Sharon: Be glad that your husband spends some fun time with your children. That's good for everyone. And you need to realize that as they grow up, your children will recognize that the day-to-day responsibilities fell on you and that you were there for them through all the difficult times.

Marilu: As I've already said, this is very similar to our family, and probably most families of my generation. My father worked six days a week and came home late every night. He was always brief and charming, while my mother, who was with us all day, was often the "heavy" with no sense of humor. Deep down, we all knew that she played the leading role and our father was the very likable supporting comedian. I really respect and admire both of the roles they played in our upbringing, and how committed they were to the same goal of our well-being.

Delayed Discipline

My husband works long hours. Often when the children do something wrong during the day, he wants me to wait until he's home so that he can discipline them. I feel that delayed discipline is useless. What do you think?

Dr. Sharon: It is unusual for a father to volunteer to be the "bad guy." But the threat "wait 'til Dad comes home" is ineffective. Threats have no place in child rearing.

Marilu: It's nice that your husband is "willing" to let you palm off some of the responsibility on him so that you're not the only "bad guy." However, I think you're right. The only effective response is an immediate one.

Dad Says Yes, Mom Says No

I expect my children to keep their rooms tidy. My husband believes that they should be allowed to keep their rooms any way they want to. When I say, "Go clean your room," they respond, "Dad says I don't have to." What do I do?

Dr. Sharon: When your children say, "Dad says I don't have to," your response should be that *you* (not your husband) are now in charge and asking them to do something. Don't get into an argument with your husband about it. He might not agree with you on this, but it is possible for you to act independently and for you to get your children to obey you.

Marilu: I am an extremely organized person, and yet, when my kids get to be around ten, I will do what my parents did with us. I will let my boys keep their rooms any way they want (with the door closed if necessary). Once every two weeks, however, I will insist that they clean their rooms enough to wipe out any conditions that might be conducive to critter breeding. When we were kids, my brothers' room was so dirty that they created some plant and insect species never before seen.

How to Be a Stepparent

My wife and her twelve-year-old daughter frequently argue without resolution. As a stepfather, I stay on the sideline, but I dislike the escalating arguments. What can I do to bring some peace to our home?

Dr. Sharon: It can be difficult to live with a stepparent, especially one of the opposite sex, so there's even more reason that boundaries be adhered to. It is possible, also, that on some level, the fight might be over you. Consequently, you are right not to interfere in their arguments and to try not to even be around when they are arguing.

Marilu: As a parent and a stepparent I have learned that the rules of the road are the same. It's best not to parent your partner's parenting.

Too Many Phone Calls?

I am a divorced father, and my seven- and eleven-year-old sons stay with me every other weekend. Their mother telephones two or three times a day to speak with them. I find it disruptive. What is reasonable in this situation?

Dr. Sharon: It is natural for a mother to want to talk to her children once or twice a day. Providing that she isn't interfering with your parenting, making unreasonable demands of the boys, or upsetting them, don't interfere. It's good for the children to know that both parents are involved in their lives and that their mother is welcome to call when they are at your house.

Marilu: Boy, you'd hate to be married to my husband. When he's away from our boys he calls so often that I have to tell him, "Nothing's changed since your last call. Let us live some life before you call again." In your case, two or three times a day doesn't sound unreasonable to me at all, especially with a seven-year-old.

When to Get Involved in Fights

My five-year-old son reported to us that he is being hit by one of his classmates. My husband taught our son that fighting is wrong and he should walk away. I think he should fight back. Who is right?

Dr. Sharon: If there is danger of his being physically harmed, notify his teacher or the school principal. Otherwise, let him work this out himself. Let him know that you understand what he is going through but that you aren't going to interfere unless he is in danger. Your resolve will strengthen his ability to deal with difficulties in life.

Marilu: If I sensed that it was just typical school-bully stuff, I would stay out of it. It would be very hard for me to do that, but I know it's probably best for my child to learn on his own how to deal with jerks like that. If he were in danger, that's a completely different story. Then I would intervene. I really hate situations like this. Bullies create so much misery in the world, but bully training really prepared me for a life in show business.

The Importance of Staying Involved

My husband and I are divorced. When my fourteen-year-old visits his father he hangs out with a teenage boy who had once stolen a walkie-talkie at a street fair and called in a phony burglar report to the police. I have forbidden my son to spend time with this boy but my ex-husband is not concerned. What should I do?

Dr. Sharon: It appears your ex-husband is going to continue allowing your son to associate with this teenager, so be pleased that your son is confiding in you. Telling your son not to have anything to do with his friend will pit your son against his father. It's best to let your son continue to see his friend and hopefully, he will continue to keep you involved in his life, so you know what's going on. If you can have open conversations, he will be able to determine for himself that there are better ways to spend his time.

WHEN LITTLE BRATS
BECOME BIG BRATS

Obviously, it is difficult to allow your spouse (or partner) to parent in ways that conflict with your own approach. However, as we have learned in this chapter, it is best to permit each other separate rules for supervision. Think of how often we adults are given conflicting orders from two different authority figures in our lives. No one is always right, just as no one is always wrong. We eventually learn to find our own answers by analyzing which set of rules works best for *us*. Letting one parent make all the rules deprives the child of understanding that there are usually at least two sides to every issue.

Here are some consequences when one parent supervises the other.

Dr. Sharon's View

Four-year-old Kevin wanted to watch a tape and his mother, preoccupied with an urgent matter, said "no." Kevin threw himself on the floor and started crying inconsolably. Kevin's father, on the phone discussing a business deal, overheard what was going on. By the time he hung up the phone and came out to the living room, Kevin had stopped crying and was cheerfully watching his tape. Aghast, the father loudly reprimanded his wife for reversing herself with Kevin. Not one, but three mistakes were made in a matter of minutes. The mother's initial "no" to Kevin was needless, reversing herself was a second mistake, and the father's reprimand (which only compounded the problem) was the third mistake.

When a lenient parent countermands the other parent's stricter approach to child rearing, their child will grow up with many false expectations. As an adult, he will expect his partner to be excessively tolerant and uncritical. Dealing with the stricter demands of life will be hard for him. Since there were always "open arms" ready to soothe him as he was growing up, nothing less than a totally sympathetic and overprotective partner will do. When the stricter of the two parents interferes with the lenient parent's approach, the consequences are similar: The child gets confused and as an adult will give his partner a "script" and "cue cards" of what loving words to say, or will "run for cover," sequestering himself from the outside world, attempting to avoid that harsh, punitive "ogre" from his early memories.

Whether a child is getting parenting approaches that complement or whose philosophies vary, he will be fine. He learns the validity of different ways of thinking and is able to react accordingly. As an adult he will expect the world to be a complex place, full of different opinions, rules, and regulations, and will know how to cope.

My parents had many different kinds of contracts between them, not all having to do with us kids. They had contracts between themselves as well. And while the point of this chapter has been to show the benefit of allowing for differences in parenting, it reminds me of certain differences in my parents that were allowed for within a particular contract. This contract, while never verbally expressed, was considered iron clad nonetheless—the Famous Rhumba Contract.

My parents' behavior at a party was always the same. My father could be found standing in the corner surrounded by any number of people, their heads thrown back in laughter at some outrageously witty and mischievous story he told, while my mom was on the dance floor (she always made sure there was dancing) with one partner after the next. Wives loved their husbands dancing with my mom because the men always picked up the latest dance step while the women got to flirt. Husbands loved their wives talking to my dad because this way they got to dance with my mom. Both of my parents had the unique talent of making every person they came into contact with feel special. This would go on throughout the evening until a prime moment toward the end of the party (like the "eleven o'clock number" in a Broadway show), when my mother, with a knowing smile, would walk over to the stereo, put on a famous Latin song (usually "Cherry Pink and Apple Blossom White") and flirtatiously move over to my father's corner. She would then put out her hand, which he would take with a sexy squeeze, and then would lead him onto the dance floor, which everyone had cleared so that the two of them could do what was known as the famous Joe and Loretta Rhumba. It was the one dance my father knew, and their moment to show everyone who belonged to whom. Remembering my parents showing off their dancing and chemistry as a couple was a beautiful way to share their differences through a binding commitment to one another. To this it is day, it is one of my favorite life-time memories.

—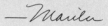

CHAPTER 5

"Cut the Drama!"

*I*n my early days of motherhood, I realized that crying is the only means of communication available to an infant trying to get his needs fulfilled. As a child gets older, temper tantrums can often become an extension of that form of communication. And if this radical, dramatic expression of need (the temper tantrum) is not converted into the more socially acceptable form of a verbal request as a child's language skills develop), it can last well into adolescence. In fact, it can become ingrained in an individual's personality for his entire life.

There are two basic components to the "temper tantrum": first, the demand or adamant request (the expression of need), and second, the reaction to the parent's response, should it be unsatisfactory to the child.

When I initially observed this behavior in my first child, I saw it as an entirely exaggerated performance of need . . . a toddler melodrama, as it were. Nicky's tantrums always seemed to be out of proportion to what was being requested. Instead of giving in to the tantrum, I would look at him with an expression of disbelief and give the referee signal for "clipping" and announce, "That's ten yards for BAD ACTING." At first he wasn't sure what to make of this other than the fact that I was not buying into his tantrum. Quite the contrary, I was dismissing it. Eventually he couldn't help but realize that he was being busted for his behavior, and he would acknowledge this awareness with his own little smile of recognition. Eventually this routine simplified to my giving him the signal for scissors (as in "rock, paper, scissors") and saying, "Cut the drama." Nicky invariably came to understand not only that I could see through his tantrums, but that there would be no conceding to this behavior. Thankfully, he is growing up to become a child of understanding and resilience. (Most of the time, anyway!)

Occasionally, every child by virtue of his own body chemistry will spin out of control and run amok. Nicky is no exception. When this occurs, my husband or I will send him to his bedroom to let the tantrum run its course. Several times I've seen him moments later, tears quelled, his enthusiastic personality restored, matter-of-factly going back to whatever he was doing, saying, "Boy, I'm glad that mood's over."

TANTRUMS:
I WANT WHAT I WANT
WHEN I WANT IT

Every child (adult, too!) wants to throw a tantrum every once in a while, but how can we as parents keep a tantrum from becoming a daily ritual? And what is the best way to handle them once they've begun? There are many different theories on this topic, but Dr. Sharon's guidelines have been very effective with my children.

Dr. Sharon's View

Brats throw temper tantrums. Because they want what they want, and they want it right away or else. Or else they will yell, slam doors, hit, scream, kick, bite, throw a toy, cry hysterically. They will sulk, get under the covers, refuse to talk, go limp. Temper tantrums come in a huge variety of shapes and sizes. But they have one thing in common. They are essentially terror tactics intended to intimidate, frighten, and control. Not surprisingly, a child who resorts to tantrums to get what he wants is usually a child who has been overindulged. (A simple test: If the parent's "no" is respected and obeyed, then the child has not been overindulged. If the parent's "no" is ignored and disregarded, the child has been overindulged.)

What all tantrum throwers need, if they have any chance of being effective, is an audience. The way their parental audience understands and handles early tantrums will determine not only what shape that particular incident will take, but whether the family is to be tortured with them for years to come. Parents are often advised that a child's

tantrum is triggered when they are inconsistent about meeting their child's needs, such as parents who agree to play a game with their child one day but don't have time to play the next day. This theory is completely wrong. Parents aren't required to be consistent about playtime. Tantrums are really triggered by parents who are inconsistent about discipline!

The parent's firmness in not giving in to tantrums helps the child's emotional development and stability. Learning that he does not achieve anything except being punished when he throws a tantrum is a lasting lesson. Without this, tantrums become life-long habits. And when they do, the child (and later the adult) no longer has the desire or the ability to control himself. And everyone in the family suffers.

If dealing with tantrums is the parent's job, preventing them is not. Parents should not walk on eggshells worried that they will trigger a tantrum. Their job is cutting off a temper tantrum at its first sign.

How to Handle a Tantrum

A raging tantrum, like a raging fire, needs to be quickly extinguished. A hug or soothing words will not do. Negotiating, bribing, giving in—none of these is a good option. Discipline is in order. The best way to deal with a child who throws a tantrum—screaming, yelling, and so on—is a firm "No!" If this doesn't work, the next step is to give the child a time-out. In a time-out, the rules are simple and not open to interpretation. The parent tells the child to go to his room for an assigned period of time. His door is shut, the lights are left on, and a monitor is placed there (if the child is young) so his parents can hear (or see) if he is in any danger of getting hurt. If the child is resistant to the idea of the time-out, his parents need to take him by his hand and lead him to his room.

In general, time-outs should be of a predetermined length so that the child knows what to expect consistently. Basically, though, the punishment should fit the crime. Use your judgment. Any further resistance should be handled by simply adding time to the child's time-out. However, threatening him with "If you don't stop crying, I'll make your time-out longer" is counterproductive. The child should not be let out of his room before his assigned time is over, not even if he behaves perfectly once he's in his room. Giving him a reprieve for good behavior is tantamount to once again letting him control the situation.

Sometimes kids innocently do things that are hysterically funny. And even though we grown-ups are dying to laugh, we can't because we know it would hurt their feelings and/or weaken our reprimand. All in all, we do a lot of "inside cheek biting" as parents. One of those times for me was when Nicky, at three years old, threw a huge tantrum after I told him that he couldn't go with Rob and me to the Hollywood Bowl to see "A Tribute to Gene Kelly" (his favorite entertainer at the time). He cried, stomped his feet, and screamed at me. He continued to sob for so long that his cries turned to hiccups. When he realized that he was getting nowhere, he picked up the phone, while still sobbing, and pretended to call the police. "Hello! Is this the police? Hi. My name is Nicky Lieberman. Could you please arrest my mother? Okay! . . . She'll be at the Hollywood Bowl tonight. Her name is Marilu Henner. I think you know her. She's the actress . . . from *Taxi*."

—*Marilu*

BRAT-BUSTERS!

Stop Whining!

Our two-year-old whines most of the time, which is unpleasant and annoying. How do I get her to stop?

Dr. Sharon: Children who whine often use their voices to evoke sympathy in their parents. Telling a child to "stop whining!" rarely works. Saying, "I will listen if you don't whine" may work for a particular incident, but the child will likely revert to whining. To break a child of whining, the parent must consistently ignore it and not succumb to giving in to what the child is whining about.

Marilu: I used to mimic. I used to bargain. Now I completely freeze and don't unfreeze until they stop whining. So far, it's working.

Distracting a Tantrum

Our baby-sitter tells us she read in a magazine that when our son throws a tantrum we should sit quietly next to him to distract him, play with his toys, and make comments about them. This is supposed to quiet him down. Do you agree?

Dr. Sharon: Magazine articles and books may offer child-rearing suggestions that are compelling reading but that make little sense. This is one! Knowing how to cut off a tantrum is confusing, especially for first-time parents. The word "no," followed by a time-out, if necessary, is still the most effective way to stop a tantrum (providing your child has learned that when you say "no" you mean it).

Marilu: When you leave a child alone to have his tantrum, and you don't interfere by distracting him, it's amazing how, without an audience, the tantrum just disappears. He *needs* that audience, otherwise the tantrum serves no purpose. My husband claims that he only screams at traffic when I'm with him in the car. There's no point in yelling with the windows rolled up if he's alone.

Tantrum in the Car

Whenever we try to secure our eighteen-month-old in his car seat, he has a temper tantrum. My husband tries to joke him out of it. This never seems effective. What should we do?

Dr. Sharon: Your husband's joking gives your child the message that he doesn't have to cooperate and suggests to him that on some level, your husband enjoys his disobedience. Be clear about your expectations when you put your son in his car seat and hope your husband will follow your example.

Marilu: I had to learn something similar to this the hard way. When Joey was very little, we would play a game with him called "Don't You Do That" and he would go ahead and do it, and we would laugh at his doing the opposite of what we said. Later, when he was a little older, we'd ask him not to do something and he'd laugh and do it anyway. After many times of *not* laughing and showing him we meant business, he finally got the message that "Don't do that!" really meant "Don't do that."

Hugging Doesn't Help

When my eighteen-month-old does not get his way, he bangs his head on a table or other piece of furniture and then proceeds to cry. Even if I pick him up and hug him to comfort him, he still takes forever to calm down. Why doesn't this work?

Dr. Sharon: As hard as it is when your child is crying and in pain, resist picking him up and hugging him. This only encourages him to throw more head-banging tantrums. When he purposely bangs his head, say "no" firmly and put him in his crib for ten minutes. As always, for his safety, since he's in his crib, leave his door open and also listen to him on the monitor.

Marilu: My friend's two-year-old son would act out by banging his head against a wall. His mother informed me that he ate and drank an excessive amount of sugar and cola. This probably contributed to his tantrums because his nervous system was so impaired from the sugar and caffeine. The tantrums subsided after he cut down on sugar and cola. I believe that diet, especially refined sugar, can play a significant role in hyperactivity.

Public Tantrums

I get embarrassed when our two-year-old daughter throws a tantrum in public, so to silence her, I give her anything she wants to make her stop. This doesn't seem to work. What can I do to stop the tantrum?

Dr. Sharon: When your daughter throws a tantrum in public, simply take her to as private a place as you can find and let her cry it out. Do not reward her because she is making a scene.

Marilu: In public, it's usually a different issue because all eyes are on you, you might be disturbing everyone's dinner, and you have to act quickly. When this happens to me, I'll usually take my child away from the situation and let them cry it out or walk around, or I'll try to distract them with something. But again, that's only in public.

Pretending Not to Hear

My seven-year-old son walks around with his fingers in his ears whenever he doesn't want to hear any instructions. I find it infuriating. What do you think? And what can I do about it?

Dr. Sharon: Explain to your son that we were meant to hear everything since we don't have earlids. Next time he does it, put him in his room for a time-out (again, leave his door open and listen to him on the monitor). His behavior is rude.

Marilu: Earlids! What a concept! The perfect solution for a whining spouse!

Threatening to Run Away from Home

My eight-year-old got angry at me and threatened to run away from home. My husband's mother said I should get a suitcase and say, "I'll help you pack your bag." Can you suggest a better way to handle this situation?

Dr. Sharon: The best thing would be to ignore his threat. If he heads for the front door, don't try to stop him. If he actually opens the door to walk out, you could say what your mother-in-law suggested, but if you suggest helping him pack, you have to follow through, and are you really prepared to do that? Another possibility is to send him to his room (door open) for a twenty-minute time-out and hope things will cool down.

Marilu: Depending on where you live, these days, I would be much too scared to let an eight-year-old walk out the door. I could *only* send him to his room for a time-out. As with any other tantrum, the "I'm running away from here" kind loses its effectiveness if no one reacts. Letting the air out of the balloon means it can't travel.

Sulking Is a Silent Tantrum

Our seven-year-old sulks when he does not get his way. How should we handle him?

Dr. Sharon: Sulking is a silent temper tantrum. Your son is reacting to not getting his way, so don't give in to him. Go on with what you're doing. If the sulking doesn't stop after about fifteen minutes, send him to his room for a time-out.

Marilu: I wish I had known about this with my first boyfriend. That guy was a professional sulker, and I spent days trying to figure out what was wrong and to win him over. Do your son's future girl-friends a favor—nip this in the bud.

The Silent Treatment

When my twelve-year-old is angry he gives us the silent treatment and we can't get him to respond to any questions. He just stares at us or into space and I get incensed. How do we change his behavior?

Dr. Sharon: The silent treatment is another form of tantrum. By giving you this treatment, he is symbolically "killing you off" (don't worry—it's only symbolic!), since you lose all power. He is using silence as a kind of weapon. But if he realizes his silence doesn't really bother you, he will give in. He will retreat from his silence the same way he would retreat from any other form of tantrum.

Marilu: Try not to take it personally and try to feel compassion for the difficult age he's at. He's getting more out of stripping you of your power when you plead with him than if you simply ignore him. I think people who use tactics like the silent treatment are so ridiculous. It is one of the most vicious weapons people use and it's such a waste of time.

"I'll Live with Dad!"

Whenever I say "no" to my thirteen-year-old daughter about anything, she gets so angry she threatens to go live with her father (we are divorced). What should I do?

Dr. Sharon: Your thirteen-year-old daughter does not have the legal right to decide where she is going to live. Simply tell her that it is not up to her to decide where she lives. At the same time, examine your own behavior and see if maybe you say "no" to her too often.

WHEN LITTLE BRATS BECOME BIG BRATS

When it comes to getting what we want, we tend to stick with strategies that work. If tantrums work, children, as well as adults, will continue to use them. In short, do not allow your children's tantrums to work from the very beginning, and your child will quickly learn not to intimidate and control everyone with their tantrums. Here are some consequences of tantrums left unchecked.

Dr. Sharon's View

Caroline stomped her feet so hard she left heel marks in the carpet. When she didn't get what she wanted, she didn't merely cry. She flopped to the ground and let out a high-pitched shriek. Then she shut up completely, slumping at her mother's feet. She offered no resistance whatsoever, which made it harder for her mother to pick her up. Her mother, tired of this almost nightly occurrence, decided that a display of opposition would stop Caroline's tantrums once and for all. With her husband's help, they picked up the silent, passive child by her arms and legs and carried her to her bedroom, telling her that she was acting like a baby and asking her to explain why she was acting this way. Instead of responding at all to this massive silent tantrum, Caroline's parents should have left her on the floor and walked away. With no attention and no opposition, Caroline would have gotten up (and given up!) by herself. Two nights later, denied a late bedtime, Caroline threw another tantrum.

Temper tantrums that go unchecked become a habit. An adult who throws loud, out-of-control tantrums has real emotional problems. He will claim he cannot help his tantrums and he is correct. His tantrums are a habit that involves his psyche and his body. Instead of him being professionally treated to eradicate the tantrums, his family cowers. Walking on eggshells around him, no one in the family dares to speak the truth. The result, sadly, is that relationships are never completely genuine. His behavior also creates real problems for his family, virtually forcing them to conform to what he is demanding or risk being further bullied and terrorized by him. It is a form of emotional blackmail.

Silent tantrums, such as sulking, are developed to perfection by the time a tantrum thrower is an adult. Family members tend to go along with this behavior, often without recognizing that they are being controlled. Sadly, the adult who throws either kind of temper tantrum is very often a depressed person. Despite seemingly getting out all his rage with his tantrum, he is unable to alleviate his depression (which is anger turned inward, so ranting and raving won't get rid of it). It's encouraging to know that a few firm "no"'s! and some short time-outs when a tantrum thrower is very young will go a long way to making sure that when he grows up, he will act like a grown-up.

CHAPTER 6

"I'm Calling Lily!"

When it comes to bringing up children, nothing raises more controversy than the various methods of discipline parents use. Methods range from extreme leniency to mental and physical abuse. Fortunately, today fewer parents hit their children. The wiser we become as a society, the more we realize that hitting is dangerous, degrading, and simply wrong, and it serves no constructive purpose. When I was growing up, hitting and humiliating were not only the norm, they were expected. I don't blame my parents or hold any grudges today because back then, nearly every mom, dad, and nun was doing it. They really didn't know any better. My siblings and I laugh about it today, but at the time, it wasn't very funny. We went to a very strict Midwestern Catholic school, Our Lady of Beat-Me-Senseless-with-the-Rosary-Beads was the name, I believe. Their methods of torture and discipline were handed down through generations of Europe's finest medieval monasteries.

I remember in first grade, after one little boy got caught sticking out his tongue at someone, the teacher forced him to keep his tongue out for the rest of the day. He was not even allowed to swallow. By the time the school bell rang, this poor boy's tongue had moss growing on it. It looked like a petri dish.

My brother Tommy, who suffered most at the hands of the Dominicans, should have been canonized for his martyrdom by the end of the third grade. He once got caught chewing gum by—I think it was—Sister Mary Milosevic. She made him kneel, fold his hands behind his back, and push a wad of gum down the entire length of the hallway—with his nose. He hasn't touched a pack of Juicy Fruit since March of '63.

Another time when he was acting out in school, the nuns taped a sign saying "I am a baby" to his chest, put a bow in his hair and a rattle in his hand, and made him parade around the entire school, classroom to classroom, for public humiliation. Most kids would have been scarred for life. My brother, a true bad-boy hall-of-famer, actually liked the attention.

My parents were not as bad as the nuns, but they weren't entirely innocent either. My mother was a part-time beautician (she ran a beauty salon out of our kitchen) and always had her weapon of choice, a hairbrush, at her side and loaded. My father was not as scary since he was too busy working and rarely home, but when he struck, he had a faster backhand than Pete Sampras.

All these tactics kept us in tow for the most part, but occasionally when serious disciplinary action was necessary, my mother used the one thing that instilled fear deep in our hearts. Our knees would tremble just from hearing the name—LILY!

She was a 300-pound German woman, a kitchen beauty salon

regular, who resided in the apartment complex next door. By day she was a cleaning lady who lived a pretty normal life, but by night, she was my mother's secret weapon against child disobedience. Ready to spring into action at a moment's notice, Lily would come over to "sit" on us. While holding the phone high above our heads, my mother would ask, "You want me to call Lily? You want her to sit on you? Is that what you want? I could have her here in five minutes." I once thought she was bluffing. I paid dearly for that assumption. When Lily arrived, she sat me down on the very hard porcelain edge of our bathtub to prepare me for the "treatment." Next, with the gracefulness of the *Queen Mary*, she turned around and slowly backed in toward the epicenter, me. And then it happened—splashdown! A 9.6 on anyone's Richter scale.

"NO" IS A COMPLETE SENTENCE

The first thing I vowed when I had kids of my own was this: No spanking, no slapping, no shaking, and definitely—no Lilys! (Besides, with all my friends off dairy, it would be hard to find someone 300 pounds.) I turned to Dr. Sharon for guidance on the subject of discipline.

Dr. Sharon's View

When it comes to raising children, some rules are crystal clear, and this is one of them: Physical punishment is humiliating and dangerous and is never an acceptable way to discipline a child. It is really just a frightening terror tactic used to assert power over a child. It is a paradox that loving parents try to relieve their children's pain when their children are sick or hurt, yet they actually inflict physical pain on these same children as a form of discipline. Whether it's a slap, spanking, or just the threat of being hit, a child will come to think of his parents as cruel and out of control. As an adult, he will recall his parents' threatening gestures—gritting their teeth, lifting their arm, or grabbing a belt or brush—as real physical assaults even though no physical contact was ever made. Getting slapped across the face, a particularly violent form of punishment, can have dire emotional and physical consequences. The eyes, the ears, the nose, the mouth, and in particular, the brain are all assaulted. And those are the lifelines, psychologically and physically, to the person's very existence. Parents who slap a child in the head are intent on harming a child in both ways.

What does work as a form of discipline? An emphatic "no" is one of the most effective words a parent can use. A few years ago, it was believed that "no" would damage a child's self-esteem, and that parents should remove the word "no" from their parenting vocabulary, replacing it with endless warnings, explanations, and negotiations. It has now become increasingly clear that these methods are pointless and ineffective. The message they give the child is that the parent is uncertain of his own rules and is not in charge. A child needs to be aware that children and parents are NOT equals and that the parent is in charge. Rules that are clearly established and boundaries that are clearly defined may make the child momentarily unhappy, but in the long run, they will make him feel safe and secure.

In most cases a child can figure out the reasons for his parent's rules and why the parent is saying "no." But in any case, the child does not need to be told *why* he should or should not do something. "You need to put your toys away" is enough. Adding, "so that tomorrow you will know where they are" is redundant. Spelling it all out and thinking for him undermine his desire to grow up and think for himself.

The Language of Parents

If parents' rules should be clear, so should their language. Unfortunately, parents often phrase commands to their children in the form of a question, such as, "Do you think you can move a little faster?" or "How about cutting it out?" This gives children the impression that they have the option to disobey. Qualifying words such as "probably," "sometimes," "unless," "hopefully," "perhaps," and "unfortunately" also render the requests ineffective and undermine commands. Take, for example, "You will *probably* be in trouble," "I *hope* you listen," "*Perhaps* you should put your toys away," "*Try* to stop bickering," "*Unfortunately* you must first do your homework." Firm statements such as "Put your toys away," "Do your homework," "Move faster," and "Cut it out" may sound harsh, but are less confusing and much more effective.

A parent should *not* have to resort to statements like "You had better," "Either . . . or," and "Unless you . . . I will . . ." Threats will only compound a child's bad behavior. And idle commands that sound like bribery or blackmail do nothing but lead to a standoff. The parent who is able to remain firm will not have to resort to threats.

There's one other approach to avoid, and that's trying to persuade a child to do something. This is an exhausting and ineffective exercise that the child, far from seeing as enlightened and loving, interprets as a form of weakness on the parent's part. Given an opening, the determined child may continue pestering until the parent gives in. From then on, the child will not take "no" for an answer. Explaining and justifying the "no" are both forms of overindulgence, which inevitably lead to negotiations and arguments. A child should not have the option to negotiate or reject what the parent tells him to do. "Do it!" are two words that say it all.

Before I knew Dr. Sharon's position on negotiating with your children, I discovered the perfect two words to get your kids to listen to you and do what you ask—"Hello Santa!"

"Hello Santa" is my shorthand for threatening and bribing your kids daily by pretending to call Santa in order to get them to do whatever you want. It's a tactic that begins right after Halloween and lasts (if you're creative enough) right up until New Year's Day (remember—you can threaten to return the toys, too.)

I know it was wrong, and I know I shouldn't have done it, but it worked *sooo* beautifully. I even had my brother call and pretend he was Santa, although he sounded more like Ed McMahon. Now they're scared of Santa and Publishers Clearinghouse.

—*Marilu*

BRAT-BUSTERS!
Punishing and Protecting

The one and only time I left my five-year-old in the care of my parents my father slapped her across her face because she said something fresh to him. This is not unusual for him. He hit me throughout my life. I disapprove of slapping or any form of physical discipline, and I cannot forgive my father for slapping my little girl. What should I do?

Dr. Sharon: As a child you were unprotected, but now you have the power to control your father's behavior toward your child. You simply must not leave her in your parents' care again. If your mother never stopped your father's abuse of you, she probably still has no control over him. Tell your five-year-old that you disapprove of Grandpa's behavior and you will not leave her there again.

Marilu: Your father is probably from a generation in which it was acceptable to slap children. Public awareness has changed a great deal on this subject, and by now your father should have changed, too. Anyone who could slap a five-year-old out of anger, especially in the face, should not be given the opportunity to do it again. I would forgive your father and move on (at least for your sake), but don't leave your child alone in his care again.

Confronting a Stranger

If you see a stranger spanking his child, is it okay to say something in order to protect the child from the humiliation?

Dr. Sharon: If you tell a stranger not to spank his child, the spanking may go underground where the child will be put in more jeopardy. If you fear the child is in psychological or physical danger, report it to the authorities.

Marilu: I understand Dr. Sharon's position on this, but it would be very difficult for me to keep my mouth shut if I saw a stranger spanking his child. Maybe someone reading this will be afraid to hit his child if he knew that I or someone else would say something to stop him.

Trashing His Room

I put a lock on my seven-year-old son's bedroom door because he kept leaving the room during a time-out. I do have a monitor

in his room. Now he gets so angry he trashes his room. He emp-
ties his drawers, throws his clothes on the floor, takes the bed
sheets off, and throws toys and books all over the room. It takes
him a week to clean it up. What should I do?

Dr. Sharon: When you open the door to your son's room and see
that he has trashed it (you may have been forewarned by the
sounds), make sure he doesn't leave his room until everything is put
back in place. Allowing him a week to clean up the mess negates the
effectiveness of the original time-out.

Marilu: This kid has the makings of a rock star. His room is only a
stepping-stone for future hotel suites. Seriously though, at age seven,
this couldn't be a new pattern. Behavior like this is established gradually. You'll have to hang tough to get him to respect you again.

Biting Baby Back?

Our eighteen-month-old son is going through the biting stage.
When he bites it really hurts. I heard that biting the baby
back—not too hard—gets the baby to realize it is painful and
he then will stop biting. It sounds barbaric to me. What do you
recommend?

Dr. Sharon: You don't teach a child not to bite by biting him, just as
you don't hit a child for hitting his brother. Inflicting physical pain
in order to teach about pain is perverse and accomplishes nothing. A
firm "no" should accomplish the desired results. If it does not, put
the baby in his crib for fifteen minutes (while observing him on the
monitor).

Marilu: This question is right up my alley. I was a major biter as a child. I didn't do it in a mean way. I was no baby Mike Tyson or anything like that. It was just my way of expressing uncontrollable love. I bit my brothers mercilessly. My mother did everything short of driving a stake through my heart to get me to stop. I wore a garlic necklace until I was twelve! Thank goodness neither of my children is a biter.

Ending a Time-Out

When I give my four-year-old daughter a time-out, should I greet her with open arms when she comes out? I want to include some positive reinforcement in a negative situation. Also, should I shorten her time-out once she calms down?

Dr. Sharon: Greeting your daughter with open arms when she comes out only softens the message she received when she was sent to her room. It's best just to go about your business, yet be pleasant. The length of the time-out should not depend on her calming down. Once it is established, stick to it.

Marilu: Giving more attention and coddling after a tantrum teaches the lesson, "Tantrums bring affection, therefore I should throw more tantrums." Put another way, "The squeaky wheel gets the oil." Stop giving your kids the "oil," and they'll stop squeaking.

Saying "No" Too Much

It seems that lately I'm always saying "no" to my two-year-old. If I say "no" too often, will it become less effective and will he tune me out?

Dr. Sharon: The word "no" will remain effective as long as you are not wishy-washy about it, in which case it will become an exercise in futility.

Marilu: You'll never say "no" more often than while your child is two. Don't worry. It gets easier as your child gets older and learns what he can and cannot do. But if you don't say "no" often, and back it up with an action that is consistent with the word, he'll never learn.

Parent and Child Aren't Equal

Our five-year-old daughter has started saying "no" to everything we ask of her. She complains that it's unfair that we say "no" to her and that she can't say "no" to us. What do we do?

Dr. Sharon: Your daughter needs to learn that parents and children are not equals. According to her reasoning, if you command her to go to bed, she should be allowed to tell you to go to bed as well. When she says "no," tell her it's unacceptable. If she repeats it, put her in her room for a time-out. In the long run, she will feel safer knowing that you are in charge and that you are the one saying "no."

Marilu: Throughout her life, your daughter will be in the same situation without her authority figures. If you set a good example, her future teachers and bosses will thank you. And your daughter will thank you for teaching her respect for, and cooperation with, people in charge.

Anticipating Bad Behavior

Whenever our six-year-old is about to do something wrong his facial expression betrays it and I warn him not to go ahead and do it. My husband thinks I should let him do it and then say "no."

Dr. Sharon: Whenever your son looks suspicious, disregard it. The word "no" should not be used when anticipating a problem (unless it's a potentially dangerous situation, like a toddler about to touch a hot stove).

Marilu: If all mothers warned their kids every time they made a facial expression, the world would have no more Jim Carreys.

Words That Help Discipline

Our pediatrician says we shouldn't use the words "good" and "bad" when we describe our four-year-old's behavior. Instead, we should use "acceptable" and "unacceptable" when disciplining him. What do you think?

Dr. Sharon: In the final analysis, consistency of discipline is what counts, not the words.

Marilu: Tell your pediatrician that this is "bad" advice and that his bill is "unacceptable."

Do Threats Work?

Threatening my four-year-old with "If you don't put your shoes on quickly then you can't go with Mommy" almost never works. I end up taking her with me because I'm a single mom and there's no one else at home. I don't know how to get her to cooperate. Please help.

Dr. Sharon: It's best not to use threats at all. But if you do threaten your daughter and she doesn't obey, you must follow through with your threat or you weaken your position from then on. Whenever you threaten your child with a consequence, make sure it is one you can carry out. One or two such threats that are followed through with consequences are probably all it will take to get her to know you're serious.

Marilu: I once told Nicky that if he didn't get ready on time, I was going to leave him at home. He didn't comply, but I was able to follow through because I could leave him at home with my husband. It broke my heart, but Nicky was able to learn the definition of consequences. (Not that staying home with my husband is facing dire consequences.)

Ignoring a "No!"

My twenty-month-old has started throwing food and utensils on the floor. He thinks it's fun to watch Mommy pick it all up. When I say "no!" he gets angry and tries to stand up in his high chair. What do I do? I am concerned he is not getting enough nourishment.

Dr. Sharon: Most likely your son ignores your "no" because he knows you don't really mean it. He may, by now, feel like it's a game. Your strategy should be to place his food in front of him and a big towel under his high chair. Make sure he's safely and securely fastened in his high chair, so he can't stand up. Let him eat and don't worry about his getting enough nourishment (unless the pediatrician disagrees). If everything in front of him lands on the floor, don't give him more food to replace it. He'll quickly learn not to throw it next time.

Marilu: When my kids started throwing their food, I took the food away so they couldn't play with it anymore. Usually children will eat when they're hungry at the beginning of the meal. When they're no longer hungry, they will start entertaining themselves by playing with their food. Try taking your son's food away when he starts playing with it. However, if he starts to shape his mashed potatoes like Devil's Tower, it might mean something. Keep your eyes out for UFOs.

Disciplining a Hitter

I read in a book that one way to help a child stop hitting other children is to tell him to take his own hand and talk to it, and say, "Hand, you should not hit people!" Do you recommend this?

Dr. Sharon: Having conversations with different parts of one's body is very odd and accomplishes nothing. The impulse to have a child talk about hitting is legitimate, but not to his hand.

Marilu: I have a friend who once went through this bizarre therapy that involved placing an article he was wearing (a belt, a shoe, a tie, and so on) on the chair next to him so that he could talk to it. I guess the object represented "him," and this was a way to physically talk to himself. The therapy worked fine until he started dating one of his shirts. . . . No, I'm sure it didn't help much. He looks back now and says, "What was I thinking?"

WHEN LITTLE BRATS
BECOME BIG BRATS

Discipline can be a complicated and emotionally charged issue. Consequently, I would like to summarize three important points in this chapter: 1) Physical and verbally abusive discipline is humiliating, debilitating, immoral, and illegal; 2) Truly effective discipline comes from the appropriate, firm, and consistent use of the word "no," complemented, when necessary, with a time-out; and 3) Weak negotiations and explanations are simply ineffective. Here are some final examples to illustrate what happens when these points are not followed.

Dr. Sharon's View

"Nathan," said his mother in a no-nonsense voice, "if I let you stay up and watch one more television show you will not get a good night's sleep and you'll be tired at school tomorrow and your grades will suffer and your health will deteriorate from the stress and you'll get kicked off the softball team and then you won't get into Harvard and you won't go to medical school and nobody will want to marry you and then you won't have a big house with a swimming pool and a three-car garage. Would you like that to happen?" Nathan's mother is saying "no" to his request to watch more television, but at the end of her narration Nathan's mind reeled from the predictions of a doomed life. Nevertheless, Nathan once again insisted on staying up another half hour to

watch his favorite show. Back to square one, for his mother's words had had absolutely no effect on Nathan. "Explaining" must take the form of telling the child it is his bedtime. Period! And a response to his insistence is "no," which is to the point and much more effective than predictions of consequences.

When parents are reluctant to say a firm "no" to their children, their children will be reluctant to obey them. Their halfhearted commands, long-winded explanations, weak threats, and mixed messages will all be ignored or disregarded by the child. The result is a confused and inconsistently disciplined child who often will grow up to be a shy, insecure adult in public and an ornery, irreverent, and difficult person at home. The child who is inappropriately and harshly disciplined, frequently spanked or slapped (particularly because the parent is in a bad mood), will later in life allow other people, even his spouse, to treat him poorly. His self-esteem will be shaky and based on other people's approval. In contrast, the consistently disciplined child is given every opportunity to grow up stable and cooperative, both at home and in the world.

He's in the Middle
of His Own Movie

Comedian Judy Toll said it best: "After years of therapy, I realized I'm the biggest piece of crap . . . that the world revolves around."

We all know them. We've all dated them. Some of us have even married them . . . twice. They're those princes or princesses who think they walk above ground (or on water) and the rest of us are merely their subjects. They believe they are starring in their own movies, and we're just the wanna-be extras hoping to get a line. I know so many people like this (especially in show business). They walk around as if they're entitled to anything. They tend to be histrionic, too. Everything that happens around them often has this sense of high drama. Nothing is ever right, and every problem is always somebody else's fault.

A guy I went out with was exactly like this. I wondered how he became such a "prince," and then I met the queen. My boyfriend's mother completely doted on her precious baby (my boyfriend), and nothing was good enough for her sonny boy. I was lucky she liked me, but it was only because she hated his last girlfriend. This guy approached every encounter as if he were doing you a favor by being there, and he put very little energy into his personal relationships. His attitude was "I'll show them," but it really evolved into "I'll show me." I saw him as a real challenge and fell madly in love with him, until I got older and wiser and moved on to healthier people.

THE CURSE OF "SPECIAL"

When I had children I swore that I wouldn't let them turn out like this. I'm always asking Dr. Sharon how to prevent this from happening. What can parents do to keep their child from becoming a person who is full of himself, yet dissatisfied and completely unaware of other people?

Dr. Sharon's View

Some children are told by their parents that they were born special and that they should always have the best. Their parents spare no energy or expense to do this, at the same time protecting them from a world that might not recognize their innate gifts. These parents, only wanting to do the right thing, have read or heard that telling a child he is special will help him develop the self-esteem and confidence he needs to grow and prosper. They believe that a child who is told this often enough will know he is loved. It's not just parents who buy into this myth—in later years, the child's teachers will probably use the same hyperbolic phrases in the mistaken belief that this will convince the child that his talents are appreciated.

And it is a myth. Praising a child excessively and indiscriminately by using superlatives like "special," "amazing," "brilliant," "extraordinary," and "gifted" will *not* create the well-loved, well-balanced child, so secure he feels he can achieve anything he sets his mind to. On the contrary, it will produce an overindulged child who feels *insecure* physically and emotionally, who will never have an accurate perspective about who he is and what his place is in the family and in society. The curse of "special" is that it gives him the most unrealistic expectations, sentencing him to a lifetime of disillusionment. A gap will always exist between his insistence that he is a genius and his less-than-superlative functioning. Yet he can't figure out why everyone around him doesn't behave as if he's special.

Furthermore, most children *know* that everything they do isn't brilliant or incredible, so they may end up confused *and* dubious about what people tell them because they can't buy into their parents' constant exaggerations.

The child who has his needs tended to and receives consistent discipline will have a far better chance of becoming successful than the coddled child who hears nothing but admiring words.

The Problem with "Happy"

Another way of indulging a "special" child is to tell him, "All I want for you is to be happy in life." This sentiment may seem harmless and loving, but it does a real disservice to a child, assigning him an impossible, unobtainable task. For happiness, as a life goal, is elusive, intermittent, often random, and unpredictable. As an adult, he will pursue one career after another, one relationship after another, never settling down and always in search of what will make him happy.

Parents who don't make happiness a goal but who concentrate on the basics—making sure their child works hard in school and takes his chores and responsibilities seriously—will produce a child whose talents and values will bring him success.

A few months ago, I had the privilege of sitting next to a wonderful woman in her sixties at a dinner party. As usual, the conversation got around to every mother's favorite topic (her children), and she told me all about her two grown daughters, who are as close in age as my two boys. When I talked about writing this book, she told me that she found the theory in this chapter particularly interesting. Her older child had been the "Golden Child" growing up, with everyone telling her through her whole life how special she was. The woman had expected her older daughter to grow up and be very successful, but, as yet, she doesn't know what she wants to do with her life and is having a hard time finding herself. Her younger daughter, however, who wasn't constantly being told she was "special" while she was growing up because her older sister was getting all the attention, is now one of the most successful women in America. Her mom told me how hard this daughter had had to work to get to where she is today. She explained that nothing came easily, but her daughter learned early in life that it takes hard work and discipline to get anywhere. The younger daughter didn't grow with the curse of "special."

—*Marilu*

BRAT-BUSTERS!

Exaggerated Praise

I heard it is good to praise a child throughout the day for all his little accomplishments. ("You buttoned your shirt—that is *wonderful!*" or "You brushed your teeth. I am so proud of you!") and that these compliments are the building blocks for self-esteem. What do you think?

Dr. Sharon: Praising a child's ordinary, everyday accomplishments burdens him with a sense of entitlement. And exaggerated praise like "You are the best," "the greatest," "a genius," "one of a kind," gives a child false expectations of what he will achieve in life.

Marilu: If a child gets the same praise for doing the dishes as he did for getting A's on his report card, it gives him less incentive to work hard for the A's next semester. When a child receives praise, he should feel truly proud that he strove for something and succeeded.

Winning

My son and I are just starting to play games together. Should I let him win most of the time in order to build his self-esteem?

Dr. Sharon: Winning all the time will not build your son's self-esteem. He will not learn to tolerate setbacks in life, and he will recognize that you are bending the truth, which sets a bad example. In life, we sometimes win and sometimes lose. Also, in the real world, other people won't let him win all the time.

Marilu: I took my kids to their friend's birthday party recently and the mother throwing the party actually said to me, "Because it's his birthday, I hope you don't mind if I let my son win all the games today." Can you imagine this? What will happen to this boy when he faces the real world and starts losing once in a while?

Too Young to Share?

My friend brought her three-and-a-half-year-old son to my home to play with my son, who is the same age. My son is an only child and he's not used to other people playing with his toys. When his friend wanted to play with his toy he started to fuss. I forced him to share because I don't want him to grow up to be selfish. Did I do the right thing, or is he too young to share?

Dr. Sharon: He is not too young to know how to share. I don't know what you mean by *forcing* him to share. Simply say "no" when he takes away a toy from his friend and return it to the friend. And make sure you set a good example since his learning to share will be reinforced by your good examples. Sharing is so important because we don't live in a vacuum. We all benefit when we share our talents, ideas, and abilities.

Marilu: One of the best children's videotapes is called "Learning to Share," from *Sesame Street.* It stars Elmo, Zoey, Big Bird, and Katie Couric. It's all about sharing and compromising. My kids learned so much from this tape that every time there's a question about sharing with each other or with friends, some phrase from this tape comes up. You might want to get this for your children. (I hear they're coming out with one called "Learning to Obey" for husbands. I can't wait!)

Too Much Birthday

In my family the "birthday child" has always been special. It was a family tradition to spend an entire week celebrating each child's birthday with a different treat each night. I'd like to continue this tradition with my children. Do you think that would be okay?

Dr. Sharon: It is overgratifying to celebrate a child's birthday for an entire week. One birthday party is enough—but not one at school, one at home, *plus* a whole week of family celebrations. A child accustomed to ongoing celebrations will later in life become depressed if his spouse and friends won't fuss over his birthday. Besides, it is narcissistic to fuss that much over anyone's birth.

Marilu: I would like to know how you do it all week. Is it fiesta night on Monday, Chinese food on Tuesday? How do you keep the spirit fresh without making everybody sick? What is the expense?

What if you have a really big family? Practically every other day would be a birthday.

On the Phone

Every time my sister and I are on the phone, her six-year-old daughter interrupts our conversation. I find this frustrating and intrusive, but my sister claims that a child's needs should always come first. Is she right?

Dr. Sharon: Your sister should have told her daughter to wait until she was off the phone instead of permitting her to interrupt. There's very little that can't wait. It is a bad lesson to teach a child that her needs always come first. She is going to grow up into a demanding adult.

Marilu: I do a lot of business on the telephone. I have made it clear to my kids that most of my time on the phone is work, and I shouldn't be interrupted unless it's important. If they didn't understand this, I would never get any work done. My children's needs are the most important thing in the world to me, and one of the things I believe they need most is a sense of other people. Deferring to them first will deprive them ultimately of sharing themselves with the great big wide world out there.

Difficult or Creative?

I heard that there is a connection between a child being difficult and being creative. Our four-year-old is a very difficult child and I find it worrisome. My husband thinks I'm overreacting, and he believes that our son's combativeness will help develop his creativity and intelligence. What do you think?

Dr. Sharon: I don't subscribe to the notion that there is a connection between a child being difficult and being creative. A self-effacing parent who has not achieved his own goals may encourage his child to be difficult, thinking that will help his child achieve what the parent has not. Your husband is actually limiting your son's creativity by encouraging him to be difficult, unleashing emotional problems.

Marilu: Oh boy! This sounds like so many guys I went to acting school with in the seventies. (Don't worry, I am not going to mention any names.) So many actors use this as an excuse for not giving up drugs or alcohol or not getting into therapy. They believe their being "difficult" is what makes them creative. Unfortunately, their emotional or substance abuse problems waste so much of their time and energy, it keeps them unemployed as actors. The key element that makes a person talented and creative is, believe it or not, talent and creativity, and perhaps even more important, discipline. Being disciplined is the opposite of being difficult.

Really Gifted

I am the mother of four and although I know that many mothers believe their children are special and gifted, my family and friends agree that my five-year-old son is a genius. I don't want my other children to be hurt by how much attention their brother gets for being so advanced, but on the other hand, I don't want to deliberately deny my special son praise just to protect his siblings. How should I handle this?

Dr. Sharon: Your children are aware that their five-year-old sibling is advanced, but constant praise will cause them to resent him and he will grow up feeling above the masses, which will land him on the psychoanalytic couch. Provide him with educational stimuli—books, classical music, and music lessons, as well as special educational programs. Leave the excessive praise out.

Marilu: My mom, the mother of six, made us all feel special and advanced, each in our own way. Your son's talent may be in the academic world, but make sure your other children's talents are not being overlooked.

Menial Jobs

> Our sixteen-year-old son has been offered a job busing tables in a neighborhood restaurant. We don't want him to do it. We would rather he not work than do a menial job that will not make use of his sharp mind. Do you agree?

Dr. Sharon: What does your son want to do? Let him decide. Collecting garbage and waiting tables are demanding jobs that require hard work and responsibility, and someone has to do them. Not all lessons are academic. If, on the other hand, he thinks he is too good or too smart for menial work, his self-perception will interfere with his creativity.

Marilu: One of the best jobs I ever had was being a waitress at a summer resort. It taught me discipline, decision-making, timing, and coordination, and it sharpened my memory. It laid the groundwork for almost every job I ever had. Menial? What's menial?

Happiness

In talking to my son the other day I happened to say, "I just want you to be happy." My husband said, "What about me? I'm not happy. I'd love to quit my job, go back to school, and study the Greeks." I'm not sure he was kidding. Should he pursue his "bliss"?

Dr. Sharon: The same way it doesn't benefit a child to pursue happiness, an adult who pursues his "bliss" will have a hard time and so will his family. None of us can pursue our bliss, except for moments here and there, unless we want to become parasitic (namely, having others taking care of our responsibilties). Pursuing "bliss" is the unrealistic ambition of an adult who was told as a child that he deserved to be happy in life.

Marilu: I read somewhere that only two percent of all people love their jobs, five percent like their jobs, and the other ninety-three percent hate their jobs! My friends in Italy seem to live a certain way so that they "work to live, not live to work." They don't necessarily like their jobs, but they all seem to have jobs, and they adjust their lifestyles to their jobs. In America, we've come to believe that we should have to work only at what we love. Real happiness in life comes from taking responsibility for yourself and your loved ones in adulthood.

The Key to Life

As I was growing up, my father repeatedly told me, "The key to life is to discover what it is you truly love to do, then find some fool to pay you for it." My question is: Where do I find someone to pay me to watch ESPN with Chee-tos and a six-pack?

Dr. Sharon: Your question is humorous, but the concept is destructive. Your father would have done a better job had he advised you to go to school and obtain a degree that would qualify you for a profession, unless you did not follow his advice and you really are a successful comedian.

Marilu: Some people are lucky enough to know at an early age what it is they truly love doing. This gives them an enormous advantage in their field. The earlier they start, the greater the potential for long-term career growth and success. Most people, however, don't discover this until they are much older, and quite a few spend their entire lives searching for the one career they think will make them happy. I basically believe your father's advice is good but he should add this: It's great to discover what it is you truly love doing . . . and the best way to discover it is to dive passionately into your education. The trick is to strive for excellence in all your subjects, not just the ones you think are interesting or have the greatest potential for being useful later in life. This way, many more avenues are explored and you'll have a better chance of finding your passion. There is no better way to explore the range of career and life possibilities at a young age than by making a commitment to your education.

Success . . . or Else

My husband is basically a loving and supportive man, but he becomes inconsolable and depressed when a colleague succeeds. He can't read of promotions or participate in celebrations honoring others in his field. What is this about?

Dr. Sharon: It sounds like when your husband was growing up he was told that *he* was the special one, and as a result, nothing short of enormous success will satisfy him. Unable to achieve success and jealous of his colleagues who are successful, he is vindictive and wants to undermine them. Since he can't do that, he turns his anger inward and becomes depressed. At home, be prepared to live with a man who is disillusioned.

Marilu: I would recommend to your husband that he get into an exercise program to help relieve *stress*. My business (show business) is a very competitive one in which the "best man" does not always win. My husband, who is a talented director, has eased the stress of show business by running every day. Maybe your husband would benefit from this as well.

WHEN LITTLE BRATS BECOME BIG BRATS

Bestowing *too* much adulation on our children is a detriment because it gives them an unrealistic perception of themselves and their abilities. Later on, they may become confused by the mixed reactions they'll receive from the rest of the world. They will also have a more difficult time improving the social, intellectual, and practical skills that are necessary to become a contributing member of society. The following is an example of what may happen when a child grows up thinking all she has to do is be "special."

Dr. Sharon's View

Mary has been told she was "special" from the day she was born. "A jewel . . . a treasure . . . our precious angel," her parents often told her. Now, at thirteen, Mary knows she is special with all her heart, although she could not begin to tell you what is special about her. All she knows is that she deserves to be treated like a princess. So, soon after the school bell rings, Mary pulls out her cell phone and admonishes her mother for being five minutes late in picking her up. Mary is mad at her music teacher, too. She didn't get the lead in the school play in spite of the fact that her father has always sworn to her that she was the best singer—head and shoulders above the others. She can't believe the housekeeper is sick today and her room is a mess (Mary never learned to pick up after herself) and she is used to everything being perfect. As if that wasn't enough, she is upset because her teachers gave her more homework than ever. Why, Mary thinks, should I have to do homework? Mary is a princess, but she has no kingdom, and the only people who treat her like royalty are her parents. When she grows up, she will still be living in an ivory tower, only, chances are, there will be no prince, no subjects, and no happiness.

Narcissism (self-love that disguises self-hate) flourishes in an adult who was treated as though he was the greatest creature, someone his lucky parents were blessed with. This child grows up very jealous of his peers, and as an adult will covet what others have. The very jealous person will hide his jealousy and reveal it in lots of different ways—by trying to make others jealous of him, by having an attractive partner, fancy clothes, and a sharp car, and so on. If all that doesn't make his friends jealous, as a last resort he undermines his friends by becoming vindictive, thereby eliminating the necessity or reason for him to be jealous of them. Lack of resilience rears its head in the jealous person— for within the family structure, living with a non-resilient person means being subjected to his endless pouting, which is oppressive to everyone near him. To make matters worse, if he turns his anger inward, onto himself, having no other outlet, he will become depressed.

Having been told how special he was, he will not tolerate a life of obscurity, pining to have his name in lights (and rarely seeing them). Sadly, his grandiosity will torture his family, but it will torture him more.

One way emotional health is measured is by a person's ability to be resilient. Ironically, *not* being told he is the greatest and the best is probably the best way to help a child become a sensible, grounded adult who knows that the only way to get praise is to do something praiseworthy and that the only way to be on top is to work from the bottom up. Such a child will tolerate disappointment much more easily as an adult—which is a great part of coping with whatever comes his way in life.

CHAPTER 8

"But I'm Not Tired!"

As I mentioned in the Preface, right from birth, I unknowingly helped Nicky develop some bad going-to-bed habits. Since the time he started to talk, he found ways to prolong the process. "But I'm not tired" became the nightly chant when he was told it was time for bed. I would remain steadfast, countering with suggestions like "Just close your eyes and count sheep." To which he'd reply, "How many?" After a great deal of protracted negotiations he would eventually tire of the process, but this ritual took a long time to reverse. By the time Joey arrived, I had found the error of my ways and allowed him to go to sleep on his own. He developed the habit of *wanting* to be left alone to go to sleep. He would actually volunteer that he was tired and that he wanted to go to bed. But once Nicky and Joey began to room together, sharing a bunk bed, Nicky's residual habits took precedence, and a new nightly ritual was born. About thirty to forty-five minutes before I want them to go to sleep I have to get them into their pajamas, have a glass of "milk" (Rice Dream, of course), brush their teeth, and snuggle down for a story, either one I read from a book or one we make up.

When we are finished playing our story game or reading a book, they usually want a little water, then "final potty," at which time Rob and I tuck them in with a kiss, turn off the light, and close their door. We then jointly pray that that will be it. Often it is. I think I indulge this ritual as much for my own need as I do for its help in getting them down. Being as busy as I am, I look forward to our quiet time together.

"The Story Game" is a game I invented to get my kids more involved than just listening to a story; it stimulates their imaginations and (I hope) tires them with a satisfying challenge. (We share a few laughs to boot!) I ask them to give me six words that will then be used in the story. For example, I'll say, "Joey, give me a color. Nicky, give me a superhero. Joey, give me a city." We go on and on until we have six different elements. (It can be anything—a food, a toy, a song, and so on.) We then proceed to make up a story, working those words into the plot. One child starts the story, then when that child is out of ideas, the story gets passed to the next person. This continues until all the words have been included and the story has come to a natural conclusion. It is a joy to witness how inventive your children can be and I feel it is a wonderful way to stimulate their imaginations as they ready themselves to enter the sleep state.

—Marilu

Nevertheless, I do have a bedtime contract, just like any other contract with my children: "When it's time to go to bed, it's time to go to bed, one tuck-in and one tuck-in *only*." This policy was established after putting up with five to ten tuck-ins per child, per night. Rob and I were determined we wouldn't give into "one more and that's it" no matter what. One night I had put the boys to bed in the usual manner and went upstairs. I no sooner got into bed when Rob and I heard the patter of two little feet down the hallway. The footsteps stopped just outside our bedroom door. There was a short pause (I'm sure it was to gather his courage), and then a faint knock. (The boys know they are not allowed to enter our room without knocking.) We tried to ignore it but the knock just got louder until finally we had to acknowledge it. "Who is it?" I asked. The tiny voice answered, "It's Joey." He opened the door and crossed the darkened room to stand next to our bed. "What do you want, Joey?" I asked matter-of-factly without turning on the light. "I need you to tuck me in," he sweetly implored. "I already tucked you in," I countered. And in the cutest voice imaginable, he replied, "I need you to tuck me in again." "But Joey, you know I'm only going to tuck you in once from now on. Now go back to bed." He stood there for a few moments assessing his options. Then finally he turned and walked down the hallway, softly whispering to himself as he went. I think it was the most difficult thing I've ever had to do as a mother. He broke my heart, and every maternal instinct in me wanted to go and pick him up, give him a hug, and tuck him in again. But I knew that would be the wrong message. By hanging tough and sticking to the contract, I allowed my three-year-old to feel his strength and independence while sending the message that my word could be trusted, and in that trust, I believe my children find security. He hasn't come up for an extra tuck-in since.

SLEEP DRAMAS

Here's what Dr. Sharon has to say about helping our children develop good sleep habits.

Dr. Sharon's View

No matter how they are being raised, all babies and all toddlers require a great deal of sleep. This shouldn't be surprising considering how much they have to learn about the world and how exhausting that job is. The newborn must learn who is who, what everything is, how to reach, how to stretch, how to ask for something, and so on. Everything involves the mind, which had been a clean slate, and the body, which had been fed by the umbilical cord. The mother has done all the thinking and all the nurturing, and now the amount of work for the baby is overwhelming. Toddlers, too, are discovering the world by leaps and bounds, mentally and physically, so it is no wonder they need a good night's sleep *and* an afternoon nap.

We spend close to a third of our lives asleep. And while sleep may be a physical activity, it has many emotional components and ramifications. The overindulged child (less motivated and ambitious) will generally require more sleep than the child who is subjected to a balance of frustration and gratification. The child whose parents erred on the side of overfrustration will generally require the least amount of sleep, growing up determined to rise with the sun and become a success.

Sleep habits are formed early. The child who obeys his bedtime will also be likely to get up on time and be ready for school. However, parents who give in to tampering with the parent-child contract and let bedtime become loose and unstructured will end up with irritable children who, in addition to being overtired, are unsure of their parents' true limits. Parents who are casual about a child not staying in his bed make a mistake, too. If the child appears in the doorway of the parents' bedroom in the middle of the night, it's important that the parent send or lead the child back to his room and then promptly return to his own bed. That is the clear contract; parents have their bed and must retain their privacy. To accomplish that, the child has to know his place in the family and in the house.

BRAT-BUSTERS!
Waking Up

My six-month-old daughter wakes up several times each night to feed. I am exhausted, so I bring her into bed to nurse her. My husband complains that he is disturbed. Should he move to another room until my daughter sleeps through the night?

Dr. Sharon: Your husband shouldn't move out of the bedroom. If he does he will start to resent your daughter even more. First she disturbs his sleep, then she takes over his place next to you in bed! What might help is changing your way of nursing. Try nursing her sitting up in a chair (safer than nursing her in bed), then put her back in her crib. There is no reason she should demand to be fed so frequently, so begin to reduce the number of feedings (just make sure she isn't still hungry if she falls asleep while she's nursing). If it's difficult for you to get up so many times a night, pump your milk during the day and your husband can give her the bottle at night. That would also strengthen his relationship with her.

Marilu: A possible explanation for your daughter's waking up to feed several times in the night could be *your* diet. Breast-feeding moms don't realize how much their own diet affects their babies.

The breast milk you give her is the result of the food you ate about eight hours earlier. Therefore, spicy foods and meals that are heavy in protein eaten eight hours before nursing her at night can affect your baby's sleep pattern and keep her awake when you most want her to sleep.

"I'm Thirsty!"

Lately my two-year-old wakes me up in the middle of the night crying for a glass of milk. I thought this would end after a night or two, but it seems to have become a ritual. How do I break him of this habit?

Dr. Sharon: Since your two-year-old drinks from a glass and no longer from a bottle, it shows he can cope with frustration. The best solution is to let him cry until he falls asleep. As heartbreaking as it may be for you and him, don't get him a glass of milk.

Marilu: The same thing happened with Joey around the same age. We were living in a New York apartment at the time, and I was really puzzled why all of the sudden he started to wake up asking for "milk" (Rice Dream), especially since he's ordinarily such a good sleeper. He seemed genuinely thirsty, drinking an entire glass two nights in a row. On the third night he woke up, I realized that the reason it was so easy for me to wake up with him was that I, too, had gotten up three nights in a row craving something to drink. What I finally figured out was that the weather had changed and the building we were living in had started heating the apartment. It was so dry, we were dying for something to drink. The next day I bought humidifiers for each of the bedrooms and Joey and I stopped waking up thirsty. Could this be the problem at your house?

Night-Light

My two-and-a-half-year-old son, who has been sleeping in the dark, suddenly has begun to wake up crying and demanding that we put on a bright light in his room. I don't know what the cause of this might be. Should we just keep a bright light in his room all night?

Dr. Sharon: It is not clear why your son suddenly insists a light be kept on all night. However, the request isn't unreasonable; many children between the ages of two and six like to sleep with a light on. Your son may have had a bad dream and can't distinguish between dreaming and reality when he wakes up. Cooperate with his request. Put a night-light in his room. If that doesn't satisfy him, leave a brighter light on. He will eventually outgrow this need.

Marilu: This also must be something that happens around two and a half, because at that age Joey made the same request. Up until then he had chosen to sleep in a room so dark, his nickname was Batty Bat. Anyway, after he requested a light, I put him to bed with one on, although week by week the light became less and less bright per his request.

Working Parents

My wife and I both work long hours and don't arrive home until about eight at night. We miss our five-year-old daughter and wish to spend some "quality time" with her, so we let her stay up until nine-thirty or ten on school nights. Our families think this is wrong and that she should be in bed by eight or eight-thirty P.M., and that we should wait until the weekend to spend time with her. What do you think?

Dr. Sharon: If your five-year-old can nap after school and is able to get up for school feeling fresh and rested, going to bed at nine o'clock is unlikely to harm her. Take your cues from her. In addition, your work ethics are impressive and set a good example for your daughter.

Marilu: My father worked every night until ten. If my siblings and I didn't stay up late, we would never have seen him. This schedule didn't adversely affect our grades or our health. If anything, it made us feel better to spend time with our dad. I grew up discovering that there is nothing wrong with children changing their schedule a little in order to spend time with their parents.

Negotiating Bedtime

My husband and I have to negotiate with our two-year-old son to go to bed. It has become an exhausting ritual. We watch his favorite tape, then tell him a bedtime story, he then insists on a bowl of cereal followed by a glass of juice. On the nights we don't have the energy to go through these rituals, he refuses to go to sleep. What should we do?

Dr. Sharon: A child must recognize that bedtime is not negotiable. Brace yourselves for his outrage once you remove one ritual each week. As hard as it is, he has to learn to live in the real world of limits and frustrations. Give him a little time to adjust to your new firmer bedtime rules and he will.

Marilu: If it were up to Nicky, he'd watch *Conan O'Brian* every night. Sometimes I say to him, "You tuck *me* in." When I say this, however, within five minutes, he's begging to be tucked in. Try it. I hope it works (and if you have any other good suggestions, send them to www.marilu.com).

Family Bed

I'm pregnant with my first child and nervous that I won't have the baby's room ready in time. My sister, the mother of a three-year-old, tells me there is no rush because the baby should sleep with us and he won't be needing his own room for a long time. In fact, her son still sleeps with her and her husband. She calls this the family bed. Although it sounds sweet in theory, I'm not sure. What do you think?

Dr. Sharon: A newborn kept in a bassinet next to his parents' bed for the first two or three months of his life is both customary and harmless. It makes sense to have the newborn close to his parents. But after that, it is best to put his crib or bassinet in another room with a monitor on so that he learns to sleep by himself—and try to comfort himself when he wakes during the night. This will foster his independence.

With the exception of newborns, children should not sleep in the same room with their parents and not in a family bed. It is a form of togetherness and symbiosis that is too emotionally loaded on many levels. A heavy answer, perhaps, but one that's important to ponder.

Marilu: The family bed is such a controversial subject for people that I devoted an entire hour to it when I had my own talk show. At the end of the show, the credits were rolling and people were still arguing. I heard stories that hour that haunt me today. There was one family of nine with seven boys ranging from four months to seventeen years that slept in the same large bed (several beds pushed together). They still did this despite the fact that one night the father awoke to discover his elbow in the throat of the four-month-old, cutting off the baby's windpipe. The father quickly got out of bed with the passed-out infant. He revived him in the bathroom before the mother woke up. If that story isn't enough to scare you away from a family bed setup, I don't know what is.

Sleeping Late

When I was a teenager I was not allowed to sleep late on weekends. My father pounded on my door yelling "Up and at 'em!" at seven-thirty on Saturday mornings. As a result of my early experience I let my son sleep until eleven A.M. on Saturdays. When my dad comes over to visit on weekends, he is appalled to find his grandson still sleeping. Am I hurting his progress in life—and am I making him lazy?

Dr. Sharon: There is a connection between a teenager's sleeping late and being lazy. Habitually sleeping late and staying up late are often signs of a teenager or adult who was overindulged as a child. It can demonstrate a disregard for others, because while he sleeps late, he hopes other people will carry on his daytime tasks and responsibilities for him.

Marilu: The body easily develops habitual sleep patterns. If you regularly sleep ten hours a day, the body will think it needs ten hours a day. It can also become accustomed to six hours. If you allow kids to sleep as much as they want, they could develop lazy sleep patterns. It is probably better to take charge and force them into good sleep habits. On the other hand, I believe some people are naturally nocturnal. They stay up very late and sleep very late.

Wake-Up Call

Our eighteen-month-old wakes up at five every morning and then he wants to play. I'm exhausted. What do I do?

Dr. Sharon: Don't blame your baby. What time does he go to sleep? If he gets nine or ten hours' sleep, he has every right to wake up at five A.M. What *you* can do is prepare a few safe toys in his crib so he can occupy himself until you get up yourself an hour or so later. Just because he wants to play at five A.M. doesn't mean you have to be included. Children who are constantly entertained will expect the parent to play with them any time of the day or night.

Marilu: If he's eighteen months old, he may be on the cusp of needing only one nap a day. I know as a mom it's hard to give up those few precious morning and afternoon hours that you are used to having for yourself, but pick your battles. If your baby is waking up before the rooster crows, it may be because he's getting too much sleep during the day. When I cut my boys to one nap a day, they started to wake up at a more humane hour.

Only Mommy

When our two-and-a-half-year-old son wakes up in the middle of the night, he only wants his mother. If I go in his room to make sure he is all right, he demands his mother come stay with him. My wife is tired of getting up. I really want to help her with the demands of our son. I can see how sleep-deprived she is and I know it's not fair for me to be the only one in the family who needs a good night's sleep, but I am at a loss as to what to do.

Dr. Sharon: It seems your wife has become the most important person in your son's life. A mother who wants to feel needed sometimes makes the mistake of training her baby to want *only* her, then eventually she starts to resent it. Here's how you can help: When your toddler wakes up in the middle of the night, neither you nor your wife should linger in his room, and as difficult as it may be for you to break him of the habit, let him cry. You can go in and check to see that your son is all right, then go back to your bed. Your wife should try to control her desire to go into the baby's room. It's better for him and means more sleep for her. Be sure to have a monitor in his room.

Marilu: The middle of the night is one of the most difficult times for parents and children. You're all tired, you're all vulnerable, and sometimes (though not often), something is really wrong. You're lucky that there are two of you to share the work of raising your son. Single parents don't have that option, so the solution has to come from getting your son to sleep through the night without needing a parent. Crying it out is really the only way to go, and after a few days, he'll know that everything is okay and he should go back to sleep by himself.

WHEN LITTLE BRATS BECOME BIG BRATS

How we sleep is one of the most important aspects of our lives because our sleep habits tend both to affect and mirror our emotional state. The long-term sleep patterns that we develop are established in infancy. When a parent doesn't help to establish good sleeping habits in a child it is a form of breaking a contract. The consequences—other than fatigue—can carry over into adulthood.

Dr. Sharon's View

Leslie's mother, on her way out to a dinner party, was speaking to her daughter in the most heartfelt mother-daughter way. She was telling Leslie what she expected of her that evening. "So if you wash up, brush your teeth, have your pajamas on by eight, and go to bed on time, then tomorrow we'll stop at Carvel's after school for a hot fudge sundae. But if your teeth aren't brushed and you're not ready for bed, then no dessert for you. Not even an ice cream sandwich at home. Do you understand?" Leslie nodded as she mulled it over. The contract Leslie's mother was proposing involved bribery. The parent-child contract cannot be part of a bargain, nor can it be conditional. "I'm going out. Your bedtime is nine o'clock," was what her mother should have said. Since children are faced with bedtime every night, negotiating implies that the child has a choice, which she doesn't (or shouldn't). Just suggesting that bedtime is negotiable filters into other areas, leading the child into thinking that maybe everything is open for discussion.

Always going to sleep late and getting up late are the most notable bad habits of the adult who was overindulged. But there are other reasons for unhealthy sleep patterns. The adult who is prone to silent temper tantrums or who is depressed may get under the covers and actually pull the covers over his head to escape responsibility or sleep fourteen hours in a row. To make it worse, if he suffers from anxiety he may be unable to fall asleep for hours. If it's a temper tantrum, he'll resist getting up and starting his day. Sleep becomes, for him, not a way of resting, but a safe haven. When the person had been overindulged, he will become angry and punitive toward whoever dares to try to get him out of bed when the sun rises. And like so many other issues of childhood (tantrums and sharing come to mind) that can be dealt with when they first come up, sleep issues don't *have* to turn into problems that persist into adulthood. When parents demonstrate a balance of fairness and firmness, possess the right knowledge, and set up the right boundaries, everyone is likely to get a good night's sleep.

CHAPTER 9

"And What Are We Going to Do About This?"

A friend of mine told me a funny story that happened when she was four years old and her new baby brother had recently come home from the hospital. One night, while their parents were downstairs watching television, my friend snuck her brother out of his crib, carried him to the top of the stairs, dangerously dangled him upside down by the ankle over the stairwell, and shouted to her parents, "And *what* are we going to do about *this*?" Of course, her parents didn't want her to drop him, so, to avoid scaring her by overreacting, they very cautiously walked up the stairs and negotiated with her to gently put him down. It was your typical sibling rivalry baby-hostage situation.

The baby brother is in his forties today, so I know he's okay. But he still won't go near any staircases with his sister. It's my favorite, although very scary, sibling rivalry story.

I love being part of a big family. I've always been proud of the fact that my five siblings and I continue to have a great appreciation and respect for one another. People ask me, "Why is it that you all get along so well?"

I believe it's because my mother never pushed or forced us to love one another. We just organically found our way into each other's hearts. We're all different and yet, between any two of us, there's a unique bond which only that pairing shares. I guess what I'm saying is that any one of us can end up sitting next to any one of the others and still feel like he's sitting next to one of his best friends. Believe me, we all gladly show up for every family event.

SIBLING RIVALRY

Growing up, we had our sibling rivalries, but I always felt that it was healthy. I loved hanging around with my older sisters. I loved hanging around with my younger siblings, too, although I was never above a good old-fashioned game of "Ditch 'Em." For those of you who don't know, Ditch 'Em is a game in which an accomplice (usually my brother Tommy) and I would cruelly and spontaneously decide to yell, "DITCH 'EM!" We would then run as fast as we could to get away from our victim(s)—usually our little sister Christal and/or our brother Lorin, the baby of the family. (You know, come to think of it, we haven't seen or heard from Lorin since 1962.) I realize now that Christal and Lorin were probably grateful to get away from us two meanies.

My parents had some great solutions for sibling rivalries, especially when we traveled in the family car and fought over who would sit next to the window. We took most of our family trips in the sixties when seat belts were just an overlooked accessory. My parents always sat in the front seat with my two younger brothers wedged between them, and my three sisters and I sat in the backseat. My parents decided the big sisters would sit by the windows on odd days, and on even days, it would be us little sisters. Because there were more odd days throughout the year, the older sisters had the advantage. This way they felt they had seniority, and we little sisters felt we were lucky even to be considered. This solution was carried out through our entire family life. When my boys started fighting over who got to do what (for example, press an elevator button or choose a book for a bedtime story), I remembered the Henner odd/even-days solution and I use it to this day.

—*Marilu*

A lot of people don't realize how many positive things come from having a big family. I find that kids from large families are better equipped to deal with the real world outside their family life. They have already learned how to deal with compromise, sharing, competition, teasing, jealousy, and, perhaps most important, "pride in teamwork." Put it this way: Who was healthier, the Brady Bunch or Dennis the Menace? (All right, I'll admit, Jan was a little screwed up, but otherwise . . .)

Here's what Dr. Sharon has to say on the subject.

Dr. Sharon's View

Parents who treat all their children the same do them a disservice because every child is different. So it follows that parents must try to tailor a balance of frustration and gratification to that particular child's needs and temperament. The parent-child contract that exists between that child and his parents is also unique (although it still comes under the heading of "I am the parent. I make the rules. You are the child. You obey them"). But if each contract is honored by the parents and the child, that in itself will go a long way toward fostering cooperative relationships between siblings.

Sibling rivalry is a volatile area where issues have to be handled with care. One of the worst mistakes parents can make is doing anything to exacerbate it, thereby creating lifetime friction and acrimony among their children. There are many opinions about what parents should do. Some authorities suggest curbing sibling rivalry by trying to acknowledge children's feelings. For example, a parent might say, "You feel your brother is doing that to irritate you, don't you?" or "You wish your sister would stop annoying you." But telling a child what he is feeling, as well-intentioned as it is, is presumptuous, intrusive, and very often off the mark.

Also intrusive and unhelpful is interfering with children who are having a disagreement or are verbally sparring. When two siblings fight, both take part in the entanglement, regardless of which one appears to be the victim. Parents who play judge and jury, attempting

to establish guilt, will get nowhere asking what happened and hearing details like "Daddy! Jordan hit me!" followed by "Why did you hit your brother?" and "Jackie broke my dinosaur game!" and "Jordan called me stupid!"

It helps to remember that most sibling fights have to do with trying to get their parents on their side. Which is why parents must try not to interfere. Simply by appearing on the scene, they unintentionally prolong the fighting. And there are no good answers to parents who ask, "Why are you being difficult?" or "Why are you upsetting your brother?" If siblings' arguments become intolerable, the best idea is to give both children a time-out.

The Firstborn

The firstborn often experiences the birth of a sibling as both an intrusion and disruption of life as he knew it. His feelings about suddenly having a new brother or sister have been likened to those of a wife whose husband one day, out of the blue, brings home another wife. The ways parents handle the new arrival greatly determines how the older child adjusts to the change. The first child, upon the birth of a sibling, is often seen by his parents as a "huge child," by comparison to the new baby. But if he remains important when a sibling is born, still getting time and attention from his parents, he will be able to tolerate the newcomer. Parents who suddenly become short or harsh with the older child or who err in the other direction by communicating their guilt at having disrupted his perfect world will cause the child's natural jealousy to become exacerbated and will make it much harder for him to accept his new brother or sister.

The way parents handled their first arrival will also affect the siblings. If the parents fawned over the older child and praised him excessively for every little thing, exclaiming, "Look what we've created! The greatest baby in the world!" it will follow that he'll have a hard time tolerating the frustration of losing his parents' undivided attention and affection. The second child, on the other hand, is born into a household where, from day one, there's someone else he has to share his parents' time and love with.

BRAT-BUSTERS!

Regressing to a Bottle

We have recently weaned our eighteen-month-old daughter off the bottle. When she sees us give our newborn son a bottle she cries for one, too. Sometimes she grabs his bottle and puts it in her mouth. What do we do?

Dr. Sharon: Your daughter is expressing her jealousy. It would be best to get her a sippy cup or a large plastic cup with colorful straws and tell her it belongs to her. Then put juice or milk in it for her.

Marilu: Nicky was eighteen months old when Joey was born and regressed in little ways, too. He wanted a bottle, wanted to be held more often, and so on. After a few days, he recognized that he wasn't the "baby" and, of course, preferred being the "big boy" and went back to his "big boy" ways.

Who Started It?

When our two children (ages six and ten) have a fight, each accuses the other of starting it. How do I find out who really started the fight?

Dr. Sharon: It doesn't really make a difference *who* started it and it's not your job to find out. You are not an attorney establishing guilt. Just remove yourself from the scene and let your children sort it out. Of course, in the case of physical fights, send them both for a time-out.

Marilu: I am grateful that my parents rarely got involved with our arguments when we were kids. We learned to verbally fight our own battles. But if you see blood or dismemberment, act quickly (think of the carpet)!

The "Gift" of Sharing

Should I force my children to share their toys, clothes, and so on, or should I leave it up to the children if they want to share?

Dr. Sharon: Urge your children to share. As to "forcing"—if you mean putting verbal pressure on them, the answer is yes. If you *don't* urge them, you are silently condoning their not sharing. One of the greatest gifts parents can give their children is the skill they need to get along and share with siblings throughout life.

Marilu: Growing up in a house with eight people, four bedrooms, and one bathroom, we were forced to share. To this day I wish we all still lived together. I really like sharing. I've always liked it. I think it teaches you how to negotiate, how to compromise, and how to respect another person's property and personal space. Some of my favorite childhood memories involve sharing. That's why my boys share a room.

To Hug or Not to Hug

Our five-year-old daughter refuses to kiss or hug her new baby brother. She insists she hates him. What do we do to encourage her to like him?

Dr. Sharon: Unfortunately, the more you encourage your five-year-old to hug and kiss the baby, the more she will experience you as partial to him. But if you don't pay too much attention to her when she announces she hates her baby brother, in time she will learn that he is here to stay and that she will have to get along with him. Her feelings are understandable. Just because he has intruded into her life (a painful reality for her to accept), she probably reasons, why should she also have to love him?

Marilu: I remember my mother always saying, "You don't have to love her because she's your sister," or "You don't have to like him because he's your brother," that kind of thing. I think that our mother gave us a lot if space not to like each other, and that's probably why we like each other so much today. Also, I think the advantage of coming from a large family is that if you are fighting with someone, there's always someone else to play with. Still, I was never forced to hug or kiss my siblings.

Equal Treatment

Whenever I buy something for my four-year-old child, the older child (age six) expects the same, even if it is just a pair of socks. Should I buy the older child socks as well, even though he doesn't need them?

Dr. Sharon: The younger child was born into a family where a sibling already existed, so from the start he was accustomed to unequal distribution of "goodies" in the family. The older child has it harder, for he has to learn to cope with his feelings of jealousy. If you, as the parent, don't act or feel guilty about not equalizing all gifts and purchases, your older child will learn to cope with his jealous feelings, and that will be a valuable lesson.

Marilu: In my family, shopping for practical things is on an as-needed basis for each child. However, if I'm away for a few days and bring home gifts, it's always for both of them.

A Gift for the Big Brother

We have requested our relatives and friends to bring a gift for our three-year-old son when they bring a gift for our new baby, for we don't want the three-year-old to feel left out. Is this overindulgence?

Dr. Sharon: Trying to eliminate jealousy from your three-year-old's repertoire of feelings will only make him vulnerable when he has to deal with jealous feelings later in life. Coping with his frustration of having people fuss over the new baby in the household will strengthen his resolve to cope with whatever difficulties life has in store. Parents who equalize gifts among their children and their friends, making certain, for example, that if the neighbor's child gets a new bicycle, their child gets one as well, prevent their child from experiencing jealousy and limit his ability to cope later in life when confronting jealous feelings—not to mention life's difficulties.

Marilu: Can you imagine in my childhood if every sibling got a present because one of us got a present? It would be six gifts—I mean, where does it end? I guess you could start by saying, "No wonder nobody has big families anymore—everyone would be using up their time buying presents."

Allowances

We give our ten-year-old more allowance than our seven-year-old. The younger says this is not fair and wants the same allowance that the older child receives. What do you recommend?

Dr. Sharon: This one is clear-cut: The older child has seniority and *should* get more. The younger child has to adjust to that fact.

Marilu: It's kind of like seniority in the workplace. The older child has been with the "company" longer, so he deserves a bigger "salary" as his "expense account" increases. Usually older kids get more privileges compared to the younger ones, but the younger kids usually get to do things earlier because the older ones have paved the way. I remember in my family, you had to be ten years old before you could wear nylons. It was a big deal for me to turn ten and wear them. When I was eleven and my younger sister Christal was nine, our older sister got married and wanted us to be junior bridesmaids. For the ceremony, we had to wear nylons . . . one whole year before Christal was turning ten! Believe me, after that ceremony was over, I tried to force her to switch to anklets for the reception.

Sibling and Friends

When our ten-year-old daughter has a friend over, her eight-year-old sister follows them around, which results in the older one calling her sister a "pest." Should I force the older one to include her younger sister at least once in a while, especially when the younger one's friends are not available?

Dr. Sharon: When older children shut out and act in a mean way to their younger siblings, they in a sense retaliate for the younger sibling's original intrusion of being born into their lives. So don't try to force inclusion. In life, some people are includers and some are excluders. If you look at families, you'll see that, understandably, younger siblings most often are *includers*, and the firstborns *excluders*.

Marilu: I really think behavior like this starts with the parents. My mom and dad were both includers; our house was always filled with a lot of people. Consequently, for the most part, my older siblings included me and I included my younger siblings. I would bet that if *you* included the eight-year-old when the ten-year-old wanted to play only with her friend, eventually they would all be playing together.

Praising Only One

Whenever I praise my ten-year-old son in the presence of his eight-year-old sister she gets uneasy, as if I'm comparing them. Should I praise him only when his sister is not around?

Dr. Sharon: The real problem may be how *much* you're praising your son. Praise can be overdone. A child whose parent praises him ad nauseam will often grow up to be an adult who will expect and insist on endless praise from the people he is close to. In this case, whenever you praise your son, your daughter feels criticized simply by being left out of the praise.

Marilu: With six children, if my mother had praised us only when the others weren't around, we never would have heard any praise from her.

Making Comparisons

We have different feelings for each of our children. How does that affect the children? I've heard that it is not a good idea to compare one child to another, for example, "Johnny gets his homework done on time, why can't you?" What is your opinion?

Dr. Sharon: It's never a good idea to compare siblings, calling attention to where one excels. Children already notice the difference between themselves and their brothers and sisters. Parents who reaffirm those differences are destructive. Each child is conceived at a different time in the parents' lives—the pregnancy is different, the father's treatment of the mother is different, and so on. The reality is, parents develop different feelings for each child and each child affects them differently.

Marilu: I believe that comparisons with siblings can rarely be done in a positive way. But oh boy, is it tempting. It's the hardest thing not to do and probably the best thing for parents to avoid. With two boys close to the same age, it would be so much fun for me to pit them against each other, especially when getting dressed or at bedtime.

WHEN LITTLE BRATS
BECOME BIG BRATS

For a number of reasons, it is best not to interfere too much with our children's relationships with one another. What can happen when parents do this? Here are some possibilities.

Dr. Sharon's View

Three-year-old Jeremy, who was much too old for a pacifier (but insisted on it anyway), suddenly spit it out and bit into the biceps of his little brother. He then calmly picked up his pacifier and put it back in his mouth, as his brother screamed in pain. Jeremy's mother stood nearby, mortified by what she had just observed. What Jeremy had witnessed just moments earlier was the sight of his mother furtively kissing his eight-month-old brother, then turning to her friend and asking, "Did Jeremy see me kiss the baby?" By trying to prevent Jeremy from feeling jealous of his brother, she was creating problems for both children. Jealousy between siblings is normal. And Jeremy will remain unequipped to deal with his feelings, resorting to hurting his brother, getting a perverse pleasure from his mother's reaction, and always resenting his brother and his mother.

Sadly for everyone, the older child—if overindulged—will grow up to see the younger not as a friend or ally but as a threat. On a more sophisticated level in adulthood, these feelings remain much the same. Long-established sibling rivalries continue to flourish and very often come to a head when the parents die. That's when the *real* fights begin, not over who had gotten more affection, but over the parents' wills—who is being treated better, who feels slighted with his inheritance. Overindulged from birth, he can never get adjusted to the competition of a sibling. The saga of siblings as they grow up is too often one of ongoing jealousy. It is a compliment to parents whose children get along with each other throughout life.

CHAPTER 10

Liar, Liar, Pants on Fire

Rob tells a story about taking my then five-year-old nephew Adam out for a banana split at the world-famous Rumpelmayer's in New York City. As he tells it, the two of them were sitting on stools at the soda fountain when Rob, in an effort to make conversation, and knowing that Adam had recently returned from visiting his grandparents in Florida, started out, "How was your trip to Florida?" The adorable and extremely bright little fella, deep into his ice cream treat, was not forthcoming with his answer. "Fine," he replied. Trying harder to find a common base for conversation, Rob went on. "You know, my grandparents used to live in Florida and I would visit them when I was your age." Without hesitation, while shoveling another spoonful into his mouth, Adam asked, "Where do they live now?" Rob was then faced with a dilemma. Not knowing what my sister Melody had already told her son about death, he was hesitant to open the issue. Instead he decided to circumvent it by creating a small deception. "They moved away," Rob answered sheepishly, hoping it would suffice. For the first time since the waitress had set the banana split down in front of him, the five-year-old stopped cold in his eating frenzy and stared directly up at Rob incredulously. "They'd be dead by now, wouldn't they?" he exclaimed. Rob, shocked that a five-year-old could be so perceptive, had no choice but to admit to Adam, "Yes, you're quite right. They are both dead."

TELLING THE TRUTH

This story is one of the best examples I can think of to demonstrate how children are never too young to distinguish truth from dishonesty. Dr. Sharon often says that the unconscious mind knows everything, and that is never more apparent than in small children. Even when a parent believes that he has done an expert job of fibbing or covering up the truth, his behavior will betray him. Children, even babies, are far more perceptive than they are given credit for. How honest should we be with our children? And how safe can we make it for them to tell the truth?

Dr. Sharon's View

Parents who are consistently truthful will raise children who tell the truth. Children who are lied to grow up sooner or later tampering with the truth. Lying to a child in an effort to spare him the frustration of dealing with the pitfalls and difficulties of life is just another form of overprotection and overgratification. For example, parents who reassure their child that they are not going out to dinner, and then sneak out once he is asleep, are doing him a disservice. Once a child is lied to, he will never fully trust that person to tell the truth.

Withholding information, such as not telling a child that his mother is expecting a baby in an attempt to protect him from the frustration of waiting months for the birth, is another form of over-protection. When told the truth belatedly, the child will be puzzled and will feel unsettled. Another form of withholding information, in an effort to protect him, is sparing him the pain of learning about death (when he asks and wants to know). Not knowing the truth, he will conjure up fantasies from which he will be rudely awakened, and his resilience will be replaced by anxiety.

Similarly, giving a child a dishonest explanation of a situation, particularly if it affects him deeply, is both deceptive and unwise. For instance: A two-year-old boy thought his stepmother was his biological mother. When he turned nine, his stepmother divorced his father, and the older siblings, who had known the truth all along, informed and consoled him. "She wasn't your real mother anyhow, so why are you so upset?" This long deception played havoc with the boy's ability to trust. And indeed, the longer the delay in truthfully answering a child's question, the greater the fall once he discovers the truth.

Clearly, not telling the truth is harmful. So is misrepresenting the truth when a child asks questions. And while giving the child honest explanations is important, this is best done when the child *asks* for the information. Most of the time, giving the child information he did not request, or giving too many details, is a mistake. In a different vein, a child who is instructed by his parents to misrepresent something—such as a family secret—is put in a painful and conflicted position. Children should not be told to misrepresent anything.

Some well-known parenting authorities believe that children lack an understanding of the difference between lying and being truthful and that their boundary between reality and fantasy is very shaky. However, it is quite the contrary. A child can absolutely distinguish between honesty, lying, reality, and fantasy. Parents need to give him credit for this and set a good example for him to follow as he grows up.

When Nicky was in preschool in New York, two of his teachers were pregnant. Nicky knew about it, but none of the other kids seemed to know because the teachers didn't want to tell them. These teachers even asked the parents not to tell their kids. But, Nicky had already figured out from their growing tummies. When one of the teachers went into premature labor and had to leave the school early in her seventh month, the school had a real dilemma on their hands. They decided it was best to tell the kids that she was sick. I found this particularly offensive. So I said to them, "Well, have we learned our lesson? Are we now going to tell them the truth about the second teacher being pregnant?" They said, "Oh no! It is way too much to tell them all at once." I completely disagree with this way of withholding information. Adults often wait until the last possible second to impart this kind of news because they're afraid that telling kids early will be too overwhelming or frustrating for them. So what? I say we should use the pregnancy experience as a way of teaching our children about patience and anticipation.

— *Marilu*

Setting a good example includes making it possible for a child to feel he can tell the truth. If a parent simply listens to whatever the child says and comments, "Thank you for telling me," he makes it safe for the child to express something he might otherwise be uncomfortable sharing. The message that the parent is giving the honest child is that he will listen without being judgmental or critical. He is not reprimanding the child in any way, but neither is he expressing his approval. He is, however, keeping the lines of communication open and giving his child permission to tell the truth.

BRAT-BUSTERS!

Confronting a Lie

Our four-year-old daughter has been lying lately. Do we confront her or ignore it?

Dr. Sharon: Confront her. Lying can become a habit. Sometimes a child lies when he picks up that one of his parents is untruthful. Be vigilant about consistently being truthful yourselves and tell your child not to lie. Once a child finds a refuge in lying, it is difficult to reverse.

Marilu: I always think lying should be nipped in the bud. Kids will try to test you with lies because they don't even understand what lying is, and they're so afraid of getting in trouble. I think it's best to make it safe for a child to tell the truth by not overreacting or overly punishing them when they tell the truth.

White Lies

How do I explain to my children the difference between "white lies" (lying to protect someone's feelings) and serious dishonesty, like cheating on a test?

Dr. Sharon: What is the purpose of explaining the difference between one type of lie and another? Why are "white lies" okay . . . because they protect another's feelings? All lies are intended to protect someone, mostly oneself. Explaining the difference between types of lies imparts unconscious condoning of lying.

Marilu: To protect someone's feelings, you don't have to tell someone a white lie, you can simply not tell them *all* of the truth. There can always be truth in what you say to them, but it doesn't have to be hurtful. You can always answer, "How do you like my new haircut?" with "That is going to grow out so nicely."

Honesty Pact

A friend had each member of her family sign an "honesty pact" evaluating his honesty during that week. Does that help children learn about honesty?

Dr. Sharon: Being honest should be taken for granted. An "honesty pact" implies that people may not be honest. Furthermore, evaluating family members' honesty may deal with the myriad ways a person can be dishonest, which makes dishonesty sound both creative and entertaining—a destructive consequence of an "honesty pact."

Marilu: There is something Orwellian-Big-Brother about this. My guess is that one family member started this in order to control the other members of the family. It's kind of strange. I know one family that keeps this enormous chart in their kitchen which they use to mark down every little dishonest and bad feeling they have, so they can later "clean up." One day during lunch, the six-year-old daughter got up and marked something on the chart. I said, "What did you do?" She said, "I just had a bad thought about my sister" (who was only four). It was so bizarre. I felt like I was eating with the cast of *Children of the Corn*. People must be allowed to have their own feelings. If I had to tell my husband every time I wanted to kill him, he would never sleep with his eyes closed again.

Don't Tell Mommy

Whenever I drop off my seven-year-old son at his mother's (we are separated) after a weekend with me, I always instruct him not to tell Mommy that "my friend" spent the weekend with us. I do this to help him spare his mother's feelings during this difficult time. Am I doing the right thing?

Dr. Sharon: It's best not to instruct your child to withhold information from his mother. It puts your child in a tough position. Your wife's feelings may be spared, but your son's relationship both with you and his mother will be compromised. Do you care more about your wife's feelings than your son's?

Marilu: This exact situation happened to a friend of mine, and when she realized that her son was withholding information, it made it very difficult for all parties involved. She found herself grilling the boy after every excursion with Dad because she knew what he was capable of doing. Once again, honesty is the best policy.

Scared to Tell the Truth

I heard the sound of my nine-year-old son falling down the stairs. I frantically rushed over as he ran to the refrigerator to put ice on his lip and his eye. After he removed the ice I could tell that he had been in a fistfight and faked the fall to explain the bruises on his face. He denied being in a fight so I don't know how to find out the truth. I'm upset not only because he is fighting in school but also because he doesn't feel he can be honest with me. How should I handle this?

Dr. Sharon: Do you make it safe for your son to tell you what is happening in his life? Could you be too hard on him? And how honest are you and your husband? Deception is learned behavior. At this point, don't try to establish the truth. Asking him questions now will feel like prying to him and won't help your relationship with him. Just be supportive.

Marilu: Your son sounds like a real character. He actually forced himself to fall down the stairs? What does he want to be when he grows up, a stunt man? His resourcefulness is interesting. I hope he can put it to better use.

Lying and Stealing

Our ten-year-old steals money from his mother's purse, and we don't know how to handle it. He also lies and denies lying. We are both honest, hardworking people, and we try to reason with him. Is dishonesty an emotional illness?

Dr. Sharon: Since both of you are honest, an emotional problem may be brewing. The time for reasoning with him is gone. You need to establish consequences for his behavior. If it continues over time, seek some professional help.

Marilu: When kids steal, it can be serious or just that innocent phase that all kids go through during adolescence. Sometimes adolescent theft, however, should not be taken lightly. All big-time thieves had to start somewhere. Most of them will tell you that they started with what was most accessible, namely stealing from their family and friends. If you determine that it's serious, treat it seriously.

Truthful About Death

At what age should a child attend funerals and wakes? Isn't it unhealthy for a child to see people grieving over the loss of a loved one?

Dr. Sharon: Protecting children from taking part in the grieving process is not recommended. Taking a child to a funeral at any age is okay, although it is preferable to wait until a child is eight or nine years old. As for wakes, once you've told him about the open casket, leave it up to him whether or not he attends.

Marilu: I went to dozens of open casket wakes by the time I was nine. Because I saw so many at such a young age, it was never really frightening for me. I never had nightmares. I think the bigger "deal" that is made about this creates a greater potential for scaring a child.

No Big Deal

I took my thirteen-year-old son and his friend to the movies the other day. His mom always gets him into the movies at the child's price. When I said, "Three adults," the friend said, "No, I only pay the child's price." My son didn't think it was any big deal and thinks that rigidity about telling the truth is ridiculous. He said Cineplex Odeon is richer than his friend's parents. Am I a stick in the mud?

Dr. Sharon: You are not a stick in the mud. You are a person of integrity. You should have insisted on paying for three adults or you would have been drawn into a dishonest situation. By paying for three adults, your son would have had the benefit of your good example.

Marilu: I have always believed that it's better to be honest about money, even when it's to my disadvantage. One time a salesgirl gave me too much change, but I didn't realize it until I had left the store. I went back to return the money, but the line was so long, by the time I had corrected the mistake, I got back to my car to face . . . a parking ticket.

WHEN LITTLE BRATS BECOME BIG BRATS

Lying creates more lying, and that lying creates even more. The cycle continues until you have a huge junk pile of lies. Unfortunately, our children often inherit these piles and create piles of their own. Here are some consequences in families that condone lying.

Dr. Sharon's View

Because Joshua's father was going to be on a business trip, Joshua's mother arranged to celebrate his fifth birthday two days late. Then, in order not to upset him, she told Joshua that his real birthday was, in fact, two days later. On the morning of his real birthday, the house-

keeper inadvertently greeted Joshua with "Happy Birthday." As a result, his teachers at school (who had been told to "pretend" his birthday was two days later) were alerted to the fact that Joshua knew the truth. The web of deception in the service of not upsetting Joshua only made him anxious and upset. He began to eye his parents and teachers with suspicion. His birthday was a miserable experience for everyone. Joshua's mother should have told him that his birthday was going to be celebrated two days late, thereby avoiding a whole string of lies and deceptions. To spare a situation she thought would frustrate her son, Joshua's mother resorted to behavior that was dishonest and far more damaging.

A child who lies because he lives in a family where honesty isn't sacred is likely to have little regard for the truth all his life. Adults who don't tell the truth tend to cheat and act deceptively. They are frequently charming people who have developed their lying skills to perfection, always hiding behind their innocent demeanor. These people often have other related problems. In adulthood, one of the most serious consequences of years of lying is promiscuity. Straying from the truth so freely and easily can pave the road for straying in marriage and not honoring contracts. Cheating in business is another adult consequence of years of lying.

Consequently, as painful as the truth may be, it helps the child to hear it from loving and forthright parents. Being truthful is one of the best ways to make a child feel secure.

CHAPTER 11

It's a Hard-Knock Life

One morning in New York when Nicky was three and a half, he was so excited because his dad was going to pick him up from preschool and take him to lunch. This was all Nicky talked about during breakfast. To him, it had the makings of a big event.

Well, about fifteen minutes before Nicky was supposed to be picked up, Rob called me at home and said that he couldn't get out of an important business meeting, and there was no way he could pick up Nicky or take him to lunch. Our poor little guy sobbed uncontrollably in the cab all the way home when I told him that his special day with Daddy was not going to happen.

Every fiber of my being wanted to protect Nicky from feeling the way he did at that moment. As a parent, you always want to protect your children from that kind of a letdown. I wanted to treat him to everything that Rob had planned, and more. I felt like taking him not only to lunch but also to an afternoon movie and a shopping spree at FAO Schwarz. Instead, I knew that it was better in the long run for him to endure the disappointment. He will have to face moments like that for the rest of his life, and I knew that facing this frustration offered a much better lesson than if I had done my best to protect his feelings. So I said, "Nicky, I know you're upset, but you know what you can tell Daddy later, when he gets home? You can say that you've now been to three schools—you've been to Oakdale [his preschool in Los Angeles], to the 92nd Street Y [his preschool in New York], and now to the School of Hard Knocks." He understood the humor, and it eased the pain a little bit. The experience was still a tough pill for him to swallow, but I could see that it was helpful for him to experience all of his feelings about it. It's the sort of lesson that fortifies his character, so that later on he won't be shattered by every disappointment.

We went home, hung out, and basically continued as we would on any other day. Now, whenever Nicky is let down about something, he'll say, "Oh boy. I guess I'm at that School of Hard Knocks again." It has become our little phrase that represents our having to adjust to "Plan B." I have talked about Plan B in every one of my books because it's such an important concept to me. I truly believe that the key to your life is how well you deal with Plan B. Plan A is what we hope for and plan for, but Plan B is what actually happens. It's our reaction to Plan B, to what *really* happens, that makes up our lives. Life is full of disappointments. It's our resilience to disappointment and how creatively we adjust to disappointment that determines how we ultimately live our lives.

*R*ecently, my boys and I set out to have a great day at the beach. As we got closer to our destination, I realized that this was a terrible idea. It was the hottest day of the year and everyone else had the exact same plan. I turned off the freeway and said, "You know what, guys? Going to the beach was Plan A, but we're now going to have a Plan B Day." We decided to explore the area where we exited and be open to any serendipitous experiences that this random neighborhood offered. Thank goodness it turned out to be a fun and safe one. We ended up having a blast. We discovered a bookstore, a craft store, a kids' gym, even a magic shop. To this day, my boys say, "Can we have another Plan B Day?" You can make all the plans that you want, but it's your adjustment to what really happens that counts most. The more resilient you are, the easier it will be to accept Plan B.

—Marilu

LEARNING TO ACCEPT DISAPPOINTMENT AND UNPLEASANT FEELINGS

Dr. Sharon taught me the following truism: If our parents shield us from painful feelings by replacing them with a pleasurable distraction, we never learn to develop the capacity to deal with emotional pain. Here are her thoughts about accepting our feelings.

Dr. Sharon's View

Parents who attempt to eliminate an unpleasant or unhappy feeling from their child's repertoire of feelings give him a very shaky foundation. Having a feeling, as unpleasant or painful as it may be, is not the problem. *Trying to get rid of the feeling is a problem.*

If a child, early in life, is deprived of experiencing such feelings as fear, jealousy, anger, frustration, and sadness, he will grow up to become anxious when he is forced to confront those feelings for the first time. A well-adjusted child needs to be in touch with all his feelings—developing new feelings while keeping old ones—so he doesn't grow up trying to escape from the realities of life.

Parents who tell their child how he is feeling, like "You feel I'm being a bad mother, don't you?" or "You wish your dad would spend more time with you," are presumptuous and intrusive, for no one knows how another person feels. Consequently, a parent who tells his child what to think and how to feel will bring up a child who will have difficulty relying on his own resources, a problem difficult to repair.

Just as a child whose parents deny him his own feelings will suffer, so will the child who is deprived of the *parent's* full range of feelings. Not having the benefit of this range of emotions, he will be inexperienced in dealing with all feelings and attitudes. It's better to witness anger and sadness, for instance, to understand that these are a part of life and aren't "bad," or feelings to be afraid of. This reasoning applies to positive emotions as well. A child who has not experienced loving feelings from his parents will not respond positively to loving communications from others. It is important for a child to be told that his parents love him and equally dangerous to tell him that they do not.

BRAT-BUSTERS!

Pacifying Feelings

Our ten-month-old frequently uses a pacifier. Are we giving him the message not to make any sounds by stuffing it in his mouth? Is thumb sucking preferable?

Dr. Sharon: Although a pacifier in a baby's mouth is visually unattractive it satisfies the baby's sucking instinct. When the baby sucks his thumb he solves his own problem. Whether thumb sucking is preferable would depend on your dentist's opinion.

I would suggest weaning a child from a pacifier after he is a year old. Otherwise he will be dependent on oral satisfaction to quell his frustrations instead of learning to tolerate them.

Marilu: By its very name, a pacifier is designed to keep a child from being frustrated, bored, or loud. When I lived in New York, I was amazed at how many kids three and four years old were sucking on pacifiers. This is probably because their living space is so close to their neighbors, and parents want their kids to be quiet. Before my children were born, I had read several studies suggesting that pacifiers and thumb sucking lead to dental problems and a dependency on cigarette smoking later in life. Because of this, I made sure that my kids rarely used pacifiers, and that was only during their first three months. I would give them one for a short moment right after breast-feeding so that I wouldn't become a "human pacifier" after they had eaten. By four months old, they were completely off the pacifier. The longer a child stays with one, the harder it is to break him of the habit. When I look at smokers I think of them as adults with pacifiers. Learning to live with uncomfortable feelings is part of life.

Anticipating Needs

My friend says that it's best to hand a baby what he wants, and that by anticipating her six-month-old baby's needs she prevents him from becoming bored, while making him feel secure. She also quickly replaces one toy with another before he gets bored or frustrated. Is this good to do?

Dr. Sharon: This approach will have the opposite effect, making the baby insecure. When the baby struggles to reach for a toy and the mother intercedes and hands it to him, the baby is deprived of the satisfaction of accomplishment. With such repeated experiences, he will expect people to anticipate his needs and hand him whatever he wants.

Marilu: I worked very hard not to be a hovering mother. I didn't want my children to think I was the *only* thing in their lives, or that everything around them had to be filtered through me. Consequently, I would put several toys and books in their crib so when they woke up they would find something to amuse themselves and to this day my kids are very good at playing by themselves, getting books on their own and playing with blocks. You can be sure someone like Robin Williams didn't have a hovering mother. He developed his talent by performing elaborate shows as a child just for himself.

Punching Bag for Feelings

I read in a magazine that a punching bag helps a child get his anger out. Do you agree?

Dr. Sharon: A punching bag is good for exercise, but not to get out anger. It symbolically represents hitting another person. Running up and down a flight of stairs or taking a brisk walk is a better release of anger. Confronting a family member and telling him "I am angry at you" will constructively release anger using language.

Marilu: Exercise works for children as well as adults. If you make exercise part of their routine while they're young, it can make all the difference in the world in how they handle stress throughout their lives.

Jealousy

My two-and-a-half-year-old daughter is very jealous when I pay attention to other children. Recently I was holding my sister's baby and my daughter insisted I put the baby down. I did so just because I didn't want to hurt her feelings. Is this jealousy normal at this age? What do I do about it?

Dr. Sharon: Jealousy is normal at an early age. When your daughter complains about your holding the baby, don't give in by putting the baby down. You don't want to prevent your child from dealing with a feeling that she will have to confront as she grows up. Her jealousy, if properly channeled (by not pacifying her), can be a constructive feeling propelling her to excel later in life.

Allowing jealousy to exist in a healthy manner curbs it from becoming too intense. This is important because emotional health is measured by a person's resilience, degree of jealousy, and intensity of vindictiveness. The resilient person will recover from an emotional injury in a brief time—in minutes or a few hours—while the nonresilient person will bemoan his emotional injury and remain unforgiving for days, years, or even a lifetime. A child who has a healthy amount of jealousy will not become overly vindictive and will develop into a resilient adult.

Marilu: My mother hated jealousy so much; she couldn't even say the word. She called it JEA instead. To her, it was the worst feeling a person could have because it was so counterproductive. She always encouraged us to take our jealous feelings and turn them into energy to improve ourselves. She always said, "You only compete with yourself."

Crying Is a Feeling

When I am about to take my two-year-old outside, I carefully put sunscreen on his arms and face. He cries and I try to calm him down by repeating, "Mommy is almost done—it's okay just one more minute," but he keeps on crying. What do I do?

Dr. Sharon: Little children will frequently complain when suntan lotion and other medications are administered. Just put sunscreen on as carefully but as quickly as you can. Don't be obsessive about it.

Marilu: This is Joey all the way. I am Polish and Greek and my husband is Jewish. Somehow Joey ended up with bright red hair and pink, almost translucent skin. He looks like a Jewish leprechaun. If I didn't put gallons of sun block on him, his skin would bubble up like a slice of pizza with extra cheese. He hates it, but too bad! I apply it fast and abundantly no matter how much he cries. When it comes to important health practices (brushing their teeth, wearing weather-appropriate clothing and sunblock, and so on), it's better not to give in to the drama.

Getting Upset and Avoiding Bad Feelings

When our six-year-old daughter breaks or loses something, my wife, to prevent our daughter from getting upset, immediately offers to replace it. Is this a good idea?

Dr. Sharon: A six-year-old should deal with the consequences of losing something. If her mother stops replacing the items, the girl will learn to recover on her own and she will learn to be resilient, not despondent over the loss. The sooner a child is permitted to feel a loss, the better she will be equipped to deal with the hard knocks of life.

Marilu: With six kids my parents would have gone broke replacing everything we broke or lost in the house. Things were always put back together with glue, tape, or safety pins. Maybe one of the best gifts you could get your daughter is a repair kit.

Masking Feelings

When our four-year-old daughter gets upset I say something funny, turning the problem into a joke so she forgets about it. It works. My mother says I do this too much and that it is not healthy to turn everything into a joke. What is your opinion?

Dr. Sharon: Occasional joking is okay. But always joking to distract your daughter from being upset will prevent her from dealing head-on with frustrating situations. In the long run she will profit by experiencing all feelings, including feeling upset, so your mother is correct.

Marilu: I often use humor to lighten situations with my sons. For example, one time Joey fell and hit his head on the ground and wouldn't let me apply a bag of ice to it until I pretended to place the bag on the ground first to take the swelling out of *it*. That cracked him up and he then let me put the ice bag on his head.

What Does a Feeling Look Like?

I've heard that a healthy way of handling an angry child is to let him draw pictures of what his "anger" looks like. Do you recommend this?

Dr. Sharon: Getting out his anger in language is good, providing it's not repetitive. But asking a child to draw a picture of what his anger looks like is not constructive or helpful. Who is to say what anger looks like? It will likely conjure up destructive images—which the child would otherwise not have thought of. I don't recommend this approach.

Marilu: I am glad I wasn't asked to do this as a child. I was a horrible artist. It is hard to express anger using bad stick figures.

Appropriate Emotions

I don't know how to help my nine-year-old daughter when she is sad and wallows in self-pity. Growing up I was not allowed to show my emotions. I don't want to do this to my daughter, but on the other hand I don't want to encourage her to wallow in self-pity. How should I deal with her?

Dr. Sharon: You may not have been permitted to show emotions, but you have empathy for your child, so, luckily, your parents' attitude did not make you an unfeeling adult. It is okay for your child to feel sad. If she wants to talk to you about it, listen to what she volunteers. Just listening will be therapeutic for her, and at the end of her story tell her she did a good job of telling you why she was upset. If she continues to wallow in self-pity, try to ignore it. If no attention is paid to her, she will soon give up wallowing in self-pity, which essentially is a silent temper tantrum.

Marilu: I think it is really important to let children feel all their emotions. I saw teachers at my sons' old preschool suppressing the kids' feelings. They would say things like, "All right now, let's take that bad feeling and put it in that drawer over there. Okay, we've said good-bye to that feeling now. It is in the drawer." That is so unnatural! And it has to be confusing and crazy-making for the kids. Not only that, but I think one day that drawer is going to get so steeped in bad feelings, it is going to lash out at the teachers like the final scene in *Raiders of the Lost Ark*.

How Parents Feel

Our seven-year-old neighbor gets picked on at home by his mother and at school by his peers. He is really not a bad kid. Why is this happening?

Dr. Sharon: A child often induces in others the predominant feeling one of his parents had for him. A child who is disliked by a parent may trigger the same feeling in his teachers, caregivers, and playmates. It's difficult to dislodge from the way the world reacts to this child. They may have to seek family counseling.

Marilu: This is a great explanation for why some people just "rub people the wrong way" and do so their entire lives. Now I understand why, when meeting someone with whom I have no prior history, I can have a feeling about him that something is just not right. I remember showing someone my first-grade class picture and they picked out a little boy they thought was cute. I couldn't believe it. It was a kid nobody liked. Upon closer examination I realized he *was* very cute but just gave off a vibe that was very unlikable.

Feeling Excluded

My eight-year-old son complains that his friends exclude him. I don't want him hurt. How do I handle this?

Dr. Sharon: If you protect your child from getting hurt, later in life he will crumble if you are not there to "hold his hand." Try not to involve yourself. It probably hurts you more than it hurts him. Listen to his complaint and tell him, "I understand." Let him figure out a way out of his own dilemma. Struggling and resolving a problem will make him stronger.

Marilu: I remember feeling hurt as a child when two of my girlfriends would pair up and exclude me, but somehow there was always some new friend to come in and take their place. Has your son explored all the possibilities in the neighborhood or he is counting on these particular friends? Maybe there is some other little boy like him who needs a friend.

WHEN LITTLE BRATS
BECOME BIG BRATS

Just as inoculations and booster shots prepare us in small doses to later fight a serious disease, frustrations and disappointments throughout childhood prepare us for more traumatic experiences as adults. What can happen when children are frequently protected from unpleasant feelings and experiences?

Dr. Sharon's View

Fearing that Johnny would be upset, his mother decided not to tell him that his dog, Scottie, was put to sleep. Instead she told him that Scottie collapsed and died naturally. Johnny was unconsciously aware of what had actually happened to his beloved dog. And at some point, Johnny would realize that he had been deceived. It would have been far better for Johnny to have been told that Scottie was very ill and that the vet recommended that the dog be put to sleep with a painless injection. And that was what had been done. Had Johnny been told, he would have dealt with his feelings at the time it happened and his questions could have been answered truthfully.

A child who was prevented from dealing with all of his emotions, having been shielded by the well-meaning, overprotective parent will, in adulthood, become extremely distressed in the face of painful feelings. This child will grow up trying to escape any unpleasant situation, shutting himself off from the real world when possible. This will be the adult who turns to some kind of sedation. Often he can't socialize without alcohol or he frequently tries to conquer his "bad" feelings by overeating or smoking.

Feelings are wonderful and important to experience; pity the child who was taught to run from them.

CHAPTER 12

Spooky, Spunky, and Sleepy

My brother Tommy has always said that the ideal mom is a balanced combination of Spooky, Spunky, and Sleepy. Spooky represents our cautious side. It's the parent who warns kids about potential dangers. A little bit of Spooky is good because it instills some protective fears in children. Too much Spooky creates unnecessary paranoia. Spunky represents the rah-rah side of parents. It's important to be Spunky to encourage kids to do their best and to be proud when they succeed. But too much Spunky makes children feel as if they're being hovered over or pushed too hard (think Mama Rose). And Sleepy is the parent who allows his kids a lot of freedom, the laissez-faire parent. The right amount of Sleepy helps develop healthy independent kids; too much Sleepy creates feelings of neglect. A good parent has a natural blend of all three.

My mother had a balanced, yet eccentric, combination of Spooky, Spunky, and Sleepy. Her Spooky side came from her bizarre rules and fears such as: You couldn't be a cheerleader because it might ruin your female organs. You couldn't live away from home your first year of college because you might commit suicide. And my personal favorite: You couldn't wear a bra until you were at least a B-cup because it might stunt your growth. (True or not, *that* seemed to work.)

Even though my mother had these odd fears, her overall temperament leaned more toward Sleepy. She didn't care whom we dated as long as he had sisters. She didn't care how close we sat to the TV as long as we didn't have the volume on while she was sleeping. (In fact, I was a grown-up before I found out that Mighty Mouse was an opera.) She didn't even care whether or not we ate breakfast (talk about Sleepy!). She had silly rules about bras, but she couldn't have cared less about breakfast. Her Spunky side was a contradiction, too. She didn't really encourage, or discourage, our getting involved in scholastic or science projects. But when it came to acting, singing, or dancing, she was the first mom to get involved. She was a real *showbiz* mom. Staying up late on school nights to watch a classic movie musical or Lana Turner film on *The Late Show* was actually encouraged. She always knew the latest dances and hippest songs. She often threw record parties where everyone had to bring a newly released 45 to attend. It was a great way for us to restock the record supply for our dancing school.

My mother may not have had the conventional balance of Spooky, Spunky, Sleepy, but it worked for me. Not all children feel that way, however. How can we as parents give our children a good balance without putting too much on them in any one category?

Dr. Sharon's View

As Marilu writes, her parents' attitudes toward child rearing, both laissez-faire and vigilant, worked well for her. Her good relationships with all her siblings, in particular, attest to her parents' intelligent approach to the family structure.

Indeed, there is great value to a parenting style that combines a healthy dose of all three approaches. A parent who acts cautiously on a child's behalf, gives him encouragement, and offers him the freedom to act independently, once boundaries are established, gives him healthy messages. In the home where a sense of humor prevails, where just being alive is a privilege, where parents' rules are respected—that is the home in which children will grow up secure and successful.

FINAL THOUGHTS FROM MARILU

I guess the best way to recognize what it is we're doing to our children is to know and understand who *we* are and why we do the things we do. Are we passing on (without even thinking about it) the behaviors and fears our parents gave us? Or are we automatically doing the opposite just to be different? Either way, we need to parent consciously in order to find the right balance.

The theories in this book are meant to help us become more aware of the things we parents do (although well intentioned) that could be holding our children back in some way and/or creating behaviors in them that are undesirable. It is information that I am finding helpful as I experience the joys and trials of motherhood. I hope that you have found Dr. Sharon's advice throughout the book to be provocative information that inspires you to look at your parenting skills from a different angle.

Just remember: As much as no one wants to raise a brat, no one wants to *be* a brat.

More Commonly Asked Questions

DEVELOPMENTAL ISSUES

Babies in a Place of Worship

My one-year-old was whimpering during the service at our place
of worship. Afterward, one of the parishoners accused our family
of being insensitive to the other worshipers. Should parents take
their babies to service?

Dr. Sharon: Alienating parents who bring their babies to a house of
worship is hypocritical. Places of worship should encourage the
entire family to attend, babies and children included.

Marilu: There are always crying babies at a service. Mass wouldn't
be Mass without a crying baby. The church I go to in Los Angeles

has an actual crying room with a glass window right on the altar. I had kids just to get a box seat at church.

Toilet Training

My son is three-and-a-half and very bright but is still not potty trained. What can I do to get him to use the toilet?

Dr. Sharon: It's a huge transition from diaper to the potty. Be patient with him. If no one shames him he will eventually, on his own, decide to use the potty. A standoff between parent and child during toilet training will only fortify the child's stubbornness.

Marilu: Is he wearing Pull-Ups or diapers? My guess would be Pull-Ups because I think we have a generation of children who are training late because of disposable pants. When a child first starts training he's given a Pull-Up and told, "They're big boy pants and not a babyish diaper." Then when we want him to move on and be totally trained, the Pull-Up is considered babyish. It's confusing. I think if children wore only diapers or real underwear they would train earlier. In your son's case, he probably wouldn't want to wear a diaper at three and a half.

Baby-Sitting Barney

My three-year-old daughter is obsessed with Barney and Disney tapes. I find myself using them throughout the day as a baby-sitter. Is it bad to allow tapes to become a major part of her life? I don't want her to become a dull couch potato.

Dr. Sharon: Exposing children to tapes such as Barney is a mostly harmless distraction. However, don't let the tapes become the major part of her life. Expose her to art and to classical music and let her express her creativity through drawing and watercolors.

Marilu: I've never been a Barney basher because he teaches children good manners. And I love *Sesame Street* because, besides being educational, it has such a great sense of humor. If you're worried about her becoming a couch potato, try supplementing Barney with Elmo-cize. However, I don't think it's a good idea for anyone to get obsessed with tapes.

Playing a Part

My four-year-old son likes to play make-believe with his thirty-year-old aunt whom he assigns the role of the pretty damsel in distress, and his uncle is the bad guy. My son is the hero who destroys the villain (his uncle). Are games like this confusing or innocent fun for a four-year-old?

Dr. Sharon: If this is the product of your four-year-old's imagination and he made up the whole scenario, that's fine. If it was inspired or thought of by his aunt or uncle, I would encourage him to be his own scriptwriter.

Marilu: This happens all the time in my family because we are all so theatrical. Our ethnic background is Polish and Greek and as kids, we used to play "Greek Gods and Heroes." I was Aphrodite, Tommy was Apollo, and my thirty-five-year-old eccentric uncle was Zeus. Because our younger brother Lorin felt bad for our Polish side, he started a rival make-believe troupe, "Polish Gods and Heroes." He was Lubaleski the Polish god and warrior, and Christal was Portky, the Polish slave girl.

Childhood Fears

Our four-year-old son is terrified when we start letting the water out of the bathtub before he gets out (as if he is afraid of going down the drain). Is this normal?

Dr. Sharon: It is not uncommon for a child to be fearful of going down the drain when the bathwater is let out. It is not an emotional problem. Take him out of the tub, then open the drain. He will outgrow these fears in time. Forcing a child to confront one of his fears is counterproductive. It will only exacerbate the fear and cause the child to mistrust his parent.

Marilu: When my children were afraid of the drain, I would take them out of the tub and let them pull the stopper. My sister JoAnn was afraid to take a bath because she was afraid that Superman might break through the wall and see her. But the funniest childhood fear was my sister Christal's. She was afraid of the painting "Whistler's Mother." (Although I think it had more to do with the poster for *Psycho* than the painting.)

No Dresses, Only Sweatsuits

My daughter, age five, refuses to wear dresses and wants to wear only sweatsuits. I let her wear whatever she wants. My husband says I'm spoiling her by not setting limits on her choices. What do you think?

Dr. Sharon: It isn't clear why your five-year-old refuses to wear dresses. I would not make an issue unless she is in kindergarten and there is a dress code, in which case, insist she conform. At other times, let her wear whatever she wants—you are not spoiling her. She will outgrow that phase.

Marilu: Friends of mine had a daughter who would only dress as a Disney character. Believe me, it's just a phase kids go through. You don't usually see a twenty-year-old Princess Jasmine unless she's auditioning for a remake of *I Dream of Jeannie.*

RESISTING OVERGRATIFICATION AND RESPECTING THE PARENT-CHILD CONTRACT

Self-Discipline

My wife feels that our children should discipline themselves. As a result, our home is chaos. What do you think?

Dr. Sharon: Children are not capable of disciplining themselves. If during the first few years of their lives children are disciplined by their parents and caretakers, they will eventually become self-disciplined, a natural outgrowth of living within parental imposed limits.

Marilu: Oh boy, does this remind me of a household I visited recently. The children were completely out of control, and their nanny took me aside begging me for a job because she had absolutely no authority over the children. The mother, who is a friend of mine, explained to me that her children are allowed to do what they want because they're little and when they are adults she will pick her battles. I would suggest you sit your wife down and make her read this book. Come to think of it I'd better send my friend this book as well.

Mom as Playmate

My eight-month-old son crawls after me and wants me to play with him all the time. At the end of each day I am exhausted. I have childproofed my home so he will be safe. How can I get him to play by himself?

Dr. Sharon: Your eight-month-old has become dependent on your constant company. Place him in a safe confined space where you can observe him and play with him for only a few minutes at a time. Be prepared for a day or two of misery for both of you as he objects, but don't give in or you will teach him one more bad lesson: namely, that if he fusses and cries, he wins.

Marilu: I can really relate to an eight-month-old boy crawling everywhere. Nicky was like the road runner at this age and could even crawl out of his Exer-saucer. I put a safety gate at the door of his baby-proofed bedroom and let him play on the floor while I worked right outside his room where I could always see him. That way he was safe, had a lot of room to explore and toys to play with, and I could get my work done and still be readily available.

No Time as a Couple

Our three-year-old daughter stays up too late and as a result my wife and I don't have time together in the evenings. I want to have an intimate relationship with my wife, but by the time she gets into bed she is too exhausted. What do I do?

Dr. Sharon: Don't try to persuade your daughter to go to bed. Endless persuasion, discussion, or negotiation won't work. Bedtime is bedtime. Once this part of the parent child contract is reinforced and honored, everyone will be happier.

Marilu: If your daughter stays up late, I'm assuming she wakes up late. What about being intimate in the morning? Or during the day when she's in preschool? Who knows? Out-of-the-ordinary times often make for some out-of-the-ordinary encounters.

Bribing to Stop Crying

My wife bribes our four-year-old to get her to stop crying. What do you think?

Dr. Sharon: Bribing, "If you stop crying I will give you . . ." will momentarily spare the child from having to deal with the predicament he is crying about, but from then on it will weaken the child's resolve to deal with similar frustrating situations without being bribed.

Marilu: Sometimes it's so hard not to bribe. Every time I do, though, I'm always sorry because the next time they cry, a bribe is expected and I'm back to square one.

When It's Good to Be "Mean"

My five-year-old's aunts, uncles, and nanny all overgratify her. I don't want to be the only "meany" in her life. What do I do?

Dr. Sharon: You may be the only "meany" in your daughter's life, nevertheless you will keep your daughter anchored in the real world. When she grows up she will recall that you were the most sensible and caring person in her early years. It's the overgratifying parent that is frequently remembered as a "meany." Grandparents, aunts, and nannies don't have the power that you, the parent, have. You cannot prevent your daughter from being overgratified by others (although you do have a say over the nannies who work for you).

Marilu: I am proud to be this kind of "meany." I feel like I must be doing a good job if my kids see me this way. When I watch my children at first get frustrated or angry about something, then overcome those problems using their own ingenuity and willpower, I know I am doing the right thing. It is okay if they get mad at me or think I am the bad guy. They never stay mad long and, even though they are too young to understand this, deep down I know they appreciate my honesty and disciplinary consistency.

Clean Plate

My husband believes very strongly that our children—ages five and eight—should finish all the food on their plates at every meal. I disagree and believe it is too rigid. What do you think?

Dr. Sharon: It is not necessary for a child to finish everything on his plate at every meal. Avoid putting a whole lot of food on his plate. If the child piles food on his own plate and then does not eat it, he is overindulged. Instruct him to take a taste before putting more on his plate.

Marilu: I think the clean plate edict is a mistake. I believe such a rule can create a compulsion to always clean your plate, which could then lead to overeating and obesity. I have a very strong opinion about the way kids should eat. I believe that they should be allowed to listen to their own natural "gauges." My kids rarely finish everything on their plate and that is fine. I do, of course, determine what they eat at home by keeping only healthy foods in the house. Simply put: I am in charge of the quality and they are in charge of the quantity.

A Break from School

About two or three times a year our six-year-old daughter likes to take a day off from school even though she is not sick. She says she "just needs a break." I let her stay home because I know that every once in a while I, too, need to take a "mental health" day from my job. My husband says this will make her irresponsible later in life. I think it is teaching her that it is okay to take care of herself. What do you think?

Dr. Sharon: I agree with your husband. Why does your daughter need a break from school? She has to learn that work can be pleasurable and does not have to be something that one needs a break from. If she is sick she stays home; otherwise she should attend school regularly. Overgratified children grow up to be adults who need frequent breaks throughout the year and look forward to the calendar of pre-holidays, holidays, and post-holidays, leaving little time for work.

Marilu: "Just needs a break"? This sounds like something kids would say because they've heard their parents say it. It's good to teach your daughter that it's okay to take care of herself, but staying home from school when she's not sick doesn't seem like a responsible way to do it.

Putting Away Toys

When I ask my six-year-old son to put away his toys, he is often resistant. I usually end up putting them away myself. It takes less time than struggling to get him to cooperate. Punishing him with time-out doesn't necessarily get his room cleaned up any faster so it is just more practical for me to do it myself. What do you think?

Dr. Sharon: A six-year-old complaining that he is too tired to pick up his toys hints at being overgratified, or that one of his parents complains about being too tired to do something around the house. It sounds like imitated behavior. If he refuses to pick up his toys, give him a time-out.

Marilu: Joey would not pick up his toys one time and it became a battle of wills. By the time I finally got him to pick up his toys I felt like Annie Sullivan. He finally picked up his toys. . . . The next thing is folding his napkin.

Piano Lessons

Our ten-year-old son is musical, but he refuses to practice the piano and wants to quit his lessons. I regret not having been "forced" to practice the piano. What do you think? It's become a battle of wills between him and me. Would you push it?

Dr. Sharon: Your son is unaware that when he grows up he will regret having given up music lessons. Find a teacher who will work with him in a way that will not discourage him. Permitting a musically gifted child to give up music lessons is a form of overgratification.

Marilu: If your son is that talented there has to be some way to tap into his being interested enough to practice. Maybe he finds the lessons dull because his music choices are limited to classical music. Take him to a music store and let him pick out music he's really interested in, and maybe the challenge of being able to play it will light that spark.

Starting Smoking

I suspect that my eleven-year-old son is smoking cigarettes. I battled this dreadful habit for twenty-five years until I quit five years ago. I don't want him to follow in my footsteps. Do I confront him?

Dr. Sharon: Your son saw you smoke the first six years of his life, and that message was imprinted in his mind. Ask your pediatrician to explain to him the dangers of smoking and show him the printed warning on each pack of cigarettes.

Marilu: Almost every smoker I know had at least one parent who smoked. Their parents' secondhand smoke has become such a part of their respiratory system that many of them are addicted to nicotine. A lot of people I know who had two parents that smoked find it almost impossible to quit. Your son is still so young that I think you should hang tough on this one. You'll probably be saving his life.

Teens on the Phone

Our teenage daughter talks to her friends on the phone when she should be doing her homework. If she is not on the phone she has the radio on. Whenever I remind her that it is homework time, she says, "We *are* talking about homework." Unless I stand by her door and listen I have no way of knowing if she is being truthful. How should we handle this?

Dr. Sharon: Don't stand by her door and listen. If your daughter's grades have not dropped since she began phone conversations with her friends or listening to the radio, don't interfere. If her grades have deteriorated, set limits about use of both the phone and radio.

Marilu: I talked a lot on the phone as a teenager, but because I was able to keep my grades up my parents never had to remind me to do my homework. Is this about homework or spending money on phone calls, or is it about something else? Maybe you could get her her own phone and she could contribute to the monthly bill if it goes over a certain amount. That might teach her responsibility and curtail her phone use at the same time.

ISSUES OF PRIVACY, SELF-ESTEEM, AND SEXUALITY

Dinnertime Nudity

My three-year-old niece took off all her clothes at the dinner table on more than one occasion. Her mother just laughs and says, "Here she goes again." I was uncomfortable. What do you think?

Dr. Sharon: The three-year-old is out of control and her mother is too lenient, which is clear from her reaction. The little girl should be told to go into her room and get dressed and return to the table. It is not cute for a three-year-old to behave in an inappropriate manner. Does one of her parents tend to be exhibitionistic? Children's behavior often betrays the parents' problems, even if the child is not consciously aware of them.

Marilu: It sounds like it has been communicated to this child that taking your clothes off is entertaining and even appealing. This mother should be really careful to communicate the right things to a little girl in terms of respecting her body.

Privacy at School

On a visit to my daughter's preschool I saw a little girl using the toilet and a little boy was urinating in a toilet next to her within her view. There were no partitions between the toilets and there was a large mirror facing them. What do you think about that?

Dr. Sharon: The fact that the school has this setup sends a bad message to the children, in a sense encouraging exhibitionism and voyeurism. It is unsettling when teachers and other professionals, who might not be trained in psychological matters, make such important psychological decisions in children's lives. Children's privacy needs to be guarded.

Marilu: This is so prevalent in the L.A. school system that I had to get myself on the cover of *Parents* in order to protest. When I saw this very situation while evaluating preschools for the first time, I ended up calling twenty-one before I found a preschool that has a potty with privacy.

Touching

When I change my two-year-old's diaper he reaches down and pulls on his penis. What is the best way of dealing with that?

Dr. Sharon: It's not uncommon for little babies to reach for their genitals when being diapered. Make certain you are not obsessive about wiping him or putting creams on him. Taking a long time to wipe and powder his genitals is sexually stimulating. Babies have sexual feelings and are reluctant to give up the "pleasure" of being diapered and becoming toilet trained. When your two-year-old pulls on his penis, refrain from saying "No" or removing his hand. Simply diaper him quickly.

Marilu: My son started pulling on his penis when he was around four months old. When I told my pediatrician, he said, "Don't worry about this. It is very normal. He'll outgrow that in about six or seven . . . decades!"

Daddy/Daughter

My husband refuses to give our one-month-old daughter a bath because he says it "feels weird." Should he force himself to bathe her so he can bond with her?

Dr. Sharon: Since your husband claims he "feels weird" when he bathes your daughter, don't insist. He may feel awkward or embarrassed because he is of the opposite sex. His feelings are not unusual and he may outgrow them.

Marilu: Your husband may also feel "weird" because he lacks the confidence that is required to give an infant a bath. Try letting him assist you. If he doesn't want to, I'm sure that your husband and daughter can bond in other ways.

Dressing Up and Dressing Older

My teenage daughter is very flat-chested. The other day when we were going to a wedding she came down all dressed up in a very tight-fitting tank dress with an obviously stuffed Wonderbra. I wanted her to take that ridiculous thing off but she was so happy and confident that I didn't want to hurt her feelings. Anyway, the staredowns and flirting from the cousins at the wedding were so obnoxious I almost got sick—unfortunately, she didn't. She's been living in her Wonderbra ever since. What should I do?

Dr. Sharon: Is your daughter thirteen or eighteen? It makes a difference. If she is under eighteen, I would tell her not to wear the Wonderbra. You still have a say about her dress code. Explain to her that beauty comes from within and a genuine person is much more appealing in the long run than a fake.

Marilu: This is a tough question because there's so much going on here: self-image, self-esteem, role playing, even cousin attraction (flirty, but safe). Your daughter is the one who thought of doing this in the first place, so it's something she feels she has control over. I would bet anything this is a phase she'll go through for a short period of time. Eventually, she'll get tired of stuffing and get into styles that look better on girls with less bosom.

Olympic Hopeful

My seven-year-old Olympic hopeful daughter just loves acrobatics and wants to enroll in the advanced tumbling program in school. Her coach leveled with me, saying she really just isn't built right for the movements involved in this sport and consequently will have difficulty in advancement as well as a higher risk of injuries. I'm so proud of her achievements and enthusiasm that even though I know the facts, I feel like signing her up. What should I do?

Dr. Sharon: Your daughter is only seven. If, however, she truly wants to proceed into an advanced tumbling class, since the coach has warned you of possible injury, discuss it with her pediatrician first.

Marilu: If I listened to every person in my life who told me I wasn't "this or that enough" to succeed, I would never have become a dancer, an actress, or an author. Make sure your daughter is safe, but applaud her enthusiasm. Besides, she's only seven and her body can change. She may also develop different passions as she grows.

TEACHING VALUES
AND LISTENING TO FEELINGS

No Compromise

I try to teach my six-year-old son the value of compromise. When-ever we disagree about something such as bedtime, unhealthy snacks, or television we always negotiate until we reach an agree-ment. Is that okay?

Dr. Sharon: Negotiating with a child until you reach an agreement gives the child the impression that he is an equal. A six-year-old must understand that the parent is in charge and that what the par-ent says goes, and as unfair as it may sound, compromises should not be a part of the parent/child relationship. A child will feel secure, and in fact you are doing him a favor, when his role is clearly defined. Although the word "compromise" generally conjures up the image of conciliatory agreement between the parent and child, it is counterproductive. The parent, at all times, must remain in charge.

Marilu: Even as a car salesman's daughter I know that negotiating with a child can be a never-ending process. A child should not learn the value of compromise by negotiating like it's a Middle Eastern bazaar, unless they want to go into the flea-market business.

Competition: Good or Bad?

The world is a competitive place. Does this mean we should encourage competition among our children in order to get them prepared for life?

Dr. Sharon: There is natural competition and a struggle for survival from day one of a baby's life. Encouraging competition is an additional burden.

Marilu: I don't think you need to encourage competition. It's there anyway. I feel it's most important not to shield or protect your child from competition with his peers—it's natural.

Honesty

We have begun to share with our children situations that required our honesty and courage and how we handled them. Is that a good idea?

Dr. Sharon: It is a good idea to share with your children personal anecdotes of how you practiced honesty and courage. Your children will profit from both the moral of the anecdote and your willingness to share these experiences with them.

Marilu: Children are such "tape recorders," and it's always amazing to hear your own language come back to you from the mouth of such a little person. They pick up everything that you do, and if you are an honest and courageous person, more than likely, they are going to be the same way. If you feel that there is some experience that they are going through that is similar to what you've been through, I think it's always good to use that as an example.

Forgiveness

How do we teach our children forgiveness, and at what age can children understand it?

Dr. Sharon: Forgiveness is not taught, it is a natural outgrowth of observing how parents behave toward each other, toward others, and toward their children. It is virtually imitated.

Marilu: My parents were very forgiving, and I think my siblings and I learned forgiveness by their example. I don't remember ever actually having explained to me the value of forgiveness.

"If Only I Had . . ."

My sixteen-year-old keeps saying "I wish I hadn't done this, I wish I hadn't done that, I should have bought this, I should have gotten the homework from someone," and so on. He constantly regrets things. How should I handle it?

Dr. Sharon: Tell your son that regret is a waste of time because it "kills" the present and it doesn't use the brain cells to be creative in present time. Tell him that the only regret he should have is that he regrets.

Marilu: After an experience, it's best to assess the situation, figure out what you can do better next time, then move on. There's nothing worse than living in regret.

Family Pets

My four-year-old wants a cat. He's too young to take care of it, and I'm concerned he may be too rough with it. Should I wait until he is older?

Dr. Sharon: Aside from asking whether it would be fair to the cat, is it fair to your son? If the cat is injured and it's his fault, it will be a destructive experience. Wait a couple of years until he understands how to take care of a pet.

Marilu: Four years old seems awfully young for a cat. Maybe you should buy him a hamster or an animal that's easier to take care of because it's in its own cage. If your son demonstrates that he can be responsible for a pet, maybe you can buy him a cat when he's five or six.

"Your Mom Is Pregnant!"

What is the best way to prepare a two-year-old and a six-year-old for a new baby brother or sister? My wife just found out she is pregnant.

Dr. Sharon: Tell the children the truth the moment you find out you are expecting. The two-year-old should be included in the information you impart. Parents who are truthful and share such information from the beginning make the family a closer unit. Share information right along, except for the feelings you have for the growing baby, or what feelings you expect the children to have for the baby when it is born. Let your children have their own reactions.

Marilu: I have the cutest picture of my son, Nicky, at age one, when I was three months pregnant with Joey. He's got a big smile on his face and he's pointing at my stomach. So, I've always been a big believer in telling kids the truth about what's going on, because their unconscious mind knows it anyway and could conjure up all kinds of strange things trying to understand it. By the time Joey was born, Nicky, then eighteen months old, felt like he was in on the whole thing because Joey was not some major shock or dirty secret.

INDEX

Marilu Henner is an acclaimed actress who has made numerous appearances in film and television and is best known for her co-starring roles on the hit television series *Taxi* and *Evening Shade.* She recently completed successful runs in productions of the award-winning Broadway musical *Chicago,* in both New York and Las Vegas, in the lead role of Roxie Hart. A promoter of mental, physical, and emotional health, Marilu is also the bestselling author of *Marilu Henner's Total Health Makeover* and *The 30-Day Total Health Make-over.* Marilu is married to producer/director Robert Lieberman. They have two children, Nicky and Joey.

Dr. Ruth Velikovsky Sharon holds B.A. and M.A. degrees from N.Y.U. and a Ph.D. from the Union Institute. She is a certified psychoanalyst and training analyst for general psychoanalytic institutes. Dr. Sharon and her son, Rafael, co-host a weekly radio talk show, *The Couch,* in New Jersey. Dr. Sharon was influenced by her father, Dr. Immanuel Velikovsky, a psychiatrist and colleague of Freud.